SOUTHWEST WISCONSIN
W9-BMQ-272

1st EDITION

Perspectives on Modern World History

The *Titanic*

1st EDITION

Perspectives on Modern World History

The *Titanic*

Daniel Gaetán-Beltrán

Editor

GREENHAVEN PRESS

A part of Gale, Cengage Learning

Farmington Hills, Mich • San Francisco • New York • Waterville, Maine
Meriden, Conn • Mason, Ohio • Chicago

Patricia Coryell, *Vice President & Publisher, New Products & GVRL*
Douglas Dentino, *Manager, New Products*
Judy Galens, *Acquisitions Editor*

WCN: 01-100-101

For more information, contact:
Greenhaven Press
27500 Drake Rd.
Farmington Hills, MI 48331-3535
Or you can visit our Internet site at gale.cengage.com.

Articles in Greenhaven Press anthologies are often edited for length to meet page requirements. In addition, original titles of these works are changed to clearly present the main thesis and to explicitly indicate the author's opinion. Every effort is made to ensure that Greenhaven Press accurately reflects the original intent of the authors. Every effort has been made to trace the owners of copyrighted material.

LIBRARY OF CONGRESS CATALOGING-IN-PUBLICATION DATA

The Titanic / Daniel Gaetán-Beltrán, book editor.
pages cm -- (Perspectives on modern world history)
Includes bibliographical references and index.
ISBN 978-0-7377-7310-1 (hardback)
1. Titanic (Steamship)--Juvenile literature. 2. Shipwrecks--North Atlantic Ocean--History--20th century--Juvenile literature. 3. Disasters--North Atlantic Ocean--History--20th century--Juvenile literature. 4. Shipwreck victims--North Atlantic Ocean--Biography--Juvenile literature. I. Gaetán-Beltrán, Daniel.
G530.T6T575 2015
910.9163'4--dc23

2014032517

Printed in the United States of America
1 2 3 4 5 6 7 19 18 17 16 15

CONTENTS

Foreword 1

Introduction 4

World Map 10

CHAPTER 1 Historical Background on the *Titanic* Disaster

1. The Enduring Cultural Resonance of the *Titanic* Tragedy 13

   Jill A. Gregg

   An encyclopedia of popular culture reviews the history of the *Titanic* disaster and its immediate impact. The author describes how the tragedy became a cultural benchmark and phenomenon.

2. How the World's Greatest Steamship Went Down 23

   Scientific American

   A 1912 article from a popular science magazine describes the construction and engineering feats of *Titanic*. It also explains various factors and decisions that contributed to the ship's sinking.

3. *Titanic* Sends Its Final Wireless Messages 32

   Great Yarmouth Radio Club

   An amateur radio organization provides an annotated transcript of the wireless transmissions between *Titanic* and other ships in the area on the night of the disaster.

4. Confusion Reigns as News of the Disaster Reaches New York **42**

New York Times

Two days before *Titanic* survivors finally reach New York, a newspaper reports on scenes around the city and at the White Star Line offices as people hear conflicting and tragic news of the event.

5. The Remains of *Titanic* Are Finally Discovered Seventy-Three Years Later **49**

Science and Its Times

The editors of a science education source provide an overview of the expeditions that located the wreck of *Titanic* using novel exploration techniques and state-of-the-art deep-sea vessels.

6. An Exhibitions Company Gains Legal Ownership of the *Titanic* Wreck **57**

Globe Newswire

A distributor of corporate and financial news reports that a US court has granted legal ownership of the artifacts recovered from the *Titanic* site to a private company.

CHAPTER 2 Controversies Surrounding the *Titanic* Disaster

1. Negligence Caused the *Titanic* Disaster **64**

US Senate Committee on Commerce

The official report of the US government investigation into the *Titanic* disaster lays out the key findings, including negligence in the design, testing, and handling of the ship. The Senate committee also recommends new and amended rules to improve ship safety.

2. The *Titanic* Investigation Raised Issues of International Law and Jurisdiction 75

House of Lords, UK Parliament

The upper house of Parliament discusses the inquiry into disaster by the US Senate. Members examine potential repercussions for their inquiry and for international laws related to ships owned by foreign companies.

3. *Titanic*'s Discovery Resulted in a Tangle of Lawsuits 83

Ricardo Elia

An archaeologist reviews the history of lawsuits related to the *Titanic* wreck, in particular the legal challenges to ownership of artifacts and access to the site, which he says are not motivated by archaeological needs.

4. *Titanic* Should Be Left Undisturbed 90

Paul Lee

A physicist and *Titanic* enthusiast discusses the limited and inconclusive information available for determining whether damage is being done to the remains of *Titanic* by human intervention.

5. Ship Designers Have Not Learned the Right Lessons from the *Titanic* Disaster 97

Edward Tenner

A writer examines the theory of conservation of catastrophe as it relates to ship design and disasters at sea. He writes that the lessons learned from *Titanic* in 1912 did not prevent the *Costa Concordia* disaster a hundred years later.

6. *Titanic* Sank Because of Weak, Poorly Made Rivets **104**

William J. Broad

A science writer reports on research proving that *Titanic*'s manufacturer used low-quality rivets that broke during the accident. If the usual, higher-quality rivets in the design had been used, the ship might not have sunk after the iceberg collision, the author claims.

7. *Titanic*'s Wireless Operators Withheld Information for Profit **111**

New York Herald

A newspaper reports in 1912 that information about the disaster was purposely kept from the public in the days after the disaster because the wireless operator who survived was promised money for an exclusive story.

8. The Passenger Evacuation on *Titanic* Reflected the Stark Class Divisions of the Time **116**

Frank Whelan

A columnist writes about the distrust and animosity between social classes evident in 1912 society and how those attitudes played a part in who survived from *Titanic*.

9. An Actress Who Survived the Disaster Began the Legend That Is *Titanic* **122**

Robert Fulford

A columnist explains how *Titanic*'s narrative tradition began less than a month after the tragedy with a silent film starring one of the survivors. Through the years, *Titanic* became a multifaceted metaphor.

10. Survivors' Own Stories Define *Titanic*'s Legacy **129**
Wade Sisson
A writer argues that the legacy of *Titanic* must continue to be defined by the tragic and human stories of those who lived through the disaster.

CHAPTER 3 Personal Narratives

1. A Teen First-Class Passenger Writes About the Night *Titanic* Sank **136**
John B. Thayer
A financial officer who was seventeen years old when he traveled on *Titanic* describes his experience of the accident and evacuation.

2. A *Titanic* Stewardess Describes the Evacuation **146**
Violet Jessup
The survivor of two major ocean liner disasters describes the night *Titanic* sank from her point of view as a crew member.

3. Survivors Share *Titanic* Escape Stories **153**
New York Post
Passengers arriving aboard *Carpathia* tell awaiting newspaper reporters their disturbing stories about the *Titanic* disaster and their rescue.

4. My Grandfather, the *Titanic*'s Violinist **158**
Christopher Ward

The grandson of a musician who died aboard *Titanic* explains researching the aftermath of the disaster and its shocking repercussions.

5. An Artist Visits *Titanic* with a Movie Crew in 2001 **164**

Ken Marschall

A man known for his detailed photorealist paintings of wrecked ships describes his participation on a deep-sea expedition with filmmaker James Cameron and his crew to make a 3D documentary.

Chronology **170**

For Further Reading **173**

Index **176**

FOREWORD

> *"History cannot give us a program for the future, but it can give us a fuller understanding of ourselves, and of our common humanity, so that we can better face the future."*
>
> *—Robert Penn Warren, American poet and novelist*

The history of each nation is punctuated by momentous events that represent turning points for that nation, with an impact felt far beyond its borders. These events—displaying the full range of human capabilities, from violence, greed, and ignorance to heroism, courage, and strength—are nearly always complicated and multifaceted. Any student of history faces the challenge of grasping the many strands that constitute such world-changing events as wars, social movements, and environmental disasters. But understanding these significant historic events can be enhanced by exposure to a variety of perspectives, whether of people involved intimately or of ones observing from a distance of miles or years. Understanding can also be increased by learning about the controversies surrounding such events and exploring hot-button issues from multiple angles. Finally, true understanding of important historic events involves knowledge of the events' human impact—of the ways such events affected people in their everyday lives—all over the world.

Perspectives on Modern World History examines global historic events from the twentieth century onward by presenting analysis and observation from numerous vantage points. Each volume offers high school, early college level, and general interest readers a thematically arranged anthology of previously published materials that address a major historical event, with an emphasis on international coverage. Each volume opens with background information on the event, then presents the controversies surrounding that event, and concludes with first-person narratives from people who lived through the event or were affected by it. By providing primary sources from the time of the event, as well as relevant commentary surrounding the event, this series can be used to inform debate, help develop critical thinking skills, increase global awareness, and enhance an understanding of international perspectives on history.

Material in each volume is selected from a diverse range of sources, including journals, magazines, newspapers, nonfiction books, personal narratives, speeches, congressional testimony, government documents, pamphlets, organization newsletters, and position papers. Articles taken from these sources are carefully edited and introduced to provide context and background. Each volume of Perspectives on Modern World History includes an array of views on events of global significance. Much of the material comes from international sources and from US sources that provide extensive international coverage.

Each volume in the Perspectives on Modern World History series also includes:

- A full-color **world map**, offering context and geographic perspective.
- An annotated **table of contents** that provides a brief summary of each essay in the volume.
- An **introduction** specific to the volume topic.
- For each viewpoint, a brief **introduction** that has notes about the author and source of the viewpoint, and that provides a summary of its main points.
- Full-color **charts, graphs, maps**, and other visual representations.

- Informational **sidebars** that explore the lives of key individuals, give background on historical events, or explain scientific or technical concepts.
- A **glossary** that defines key terms, as needed.
- A **chronology** of important dates preceding, during, and immediately following the event.
- A **bibliography** of additional books, periodicals, and websites for further research.
- A comprehensive **subject index** that offers access to people, places, and events cited in the text.

Perspectives on Modern World History is designed for a broad spectrum of readers who want to learn more about not only history but also current events, political science, government, international relations, and sociology—students doing research for class assignments or debates, teachers and faculty seeking to supplement course materials, and others wanting to improve their understanding of history. Each volume of Perspectives on Modern World History is designed to illuminate a complicated event, to spark debate, and to show the human perspective behind the world's most significant happenings of recent decades.

INTRODUCTION

Named for the immortal and powerful giants of Greek mythology, RMS *Titanic* occupies a similarly outsized place in history. Its name is invoked as a stand-in for opulence, hubris, and doom—but also romance, ingenuity, and progress. It's been called the Wonder Ship, the Ship of Dreams, the Millionaire's Special, the Floating Palace, the Last Word in Luxury, and the Unsinkable Ship. It gave the world a "night to remember" and became part of aphorisms about inevitable failure and catastrophe.

The salient facts are well known. *Titanic* was large. It was luxurious. It was a technological leap forward. Its maiden voyage was a newsworthy event, and many rich and famous people were on board. It hit an iceberg and sank, killing more than 1,500 passengers. A story about human triumph turned into a horrific and senseless tragedy.

Titanic was in fact very large. It was one of three sister ships developed simultaneously by White Star Line. The company was based in Liverpool, England, and was at the time owned by the International Mercantile Marine Company, a conglomerate owned by American industrialist J.P. Morgan. *Titanic* was 882 feet long, weighed 46,328 tons, and its engines generated 59,000 horsepower. It could hold about 2,600 passengers and 900 crew members. It featured a center propeller that was 16.5 feet long and weighed 17 tons. The wing propellers were 23.5 feet and 38 tons, dwarfing many times over the men who built the ship at Harland and Wolff, the ship's manufacturer in Belfast, Ireland.

At its most basic, however, *Titanic* was a ship on a commercial passenger line meant for the efficient transport of large numbers of people across the ocean. On its maiden voyage, *Titanic* was under capacity and carried 1,316 passengers—706 in third class, 325 in first class, and 285 in second class—and 913 crew members. More than half of *Titanic*'s passengers were traveling in third class, also called steerage, but only a quarter of them survived. In contrast, 60 percent of those traveling in first class survived.[1]

Poor immigrants leaving Europe to seek a more prosperous life in the United States were the revenue engine that created the demand for super-large ocean liners in the early twentieth century. Two million people made the trip across the Atlantic in 1912 alone. The need to capture that business was the reason White Star Line decided to build the three largest ocean liners ever, beginning in 1908. The richly carved woods, crystal chandeliers, fine linens, and excellent food and service were meant to differentiate its product from its closest competitors. White Star Line's most important rival, Cunard, owned the *Lusitania* and the *Mauretania*, which held the record in transatlantic crossing speed for almost twenty years. The faster ships could not provide the high level of passenger amenities that White Star envisioned.[2]

People of the early twentieth century—not unlike those of the early twenty-first century—were fascinated with the era's new technologies, which were replacing older, slower ways of doing things. White Star Line fed this desire for novelty by outfitting first-class suites on *Titanic* with telephones, heaters, steward call bells, table fans, and electric air blowers. An important differentiator for *Titanic* was also its sturdiness and quiet: Neither the motion of the ship as it rushed across the ocean nor the noise of its huge engines could be felt on deck or in the rooms inside.

The most fateful design decision, however, was lifeboat capacity. At the time, lifeboats were intended to ferry passengers from a sinking ship to a rescue ship, not to save the entire ship's population. *Titanic*'s lifeboats could carry about a third of the total passenger capacity and actually exceeded what was legally required in Great Britain at the time. The process of evacuation contributed to the loss of life. Many of the initial boats were lowered half full. At the beginning, passengers were even reluctant to leave, unable or unwilling to believe that the ship was in a dire emergency and would actually sink. Tragically, doors and hatches separating the lower class sections from the top deck were locked during part of the process to prevent third-class passengers from storming the deck. An unfortunate but generally accepted assumption was that the poor and the immigrants in steerage would turn into an uncontrollable mob at the slightest provocation.

The public's anticipation and curiosity about the luxuries and great size of *Titanic* are similar to the more recent excitement over the Airbus A380. The trouble-plagued airplane is the largest passenger airliner in the world, and the first-class accommodations on several airlines are reportedly the most luxurious ever attempted in commercial air travel. But, as on *Titanic*, most passengers who will board an A380 will never see first class.

The most advanced design features on *Titanic* failed to deliver on their promise. The ship was designed with sixteen watertight compartments with doors that could be closed and sealed from the bridge. The feature was intended to make the ship resistant to sinking and was designed so that up to two compartments could flood without the additional water weight sinking the ship. The collision with the iceberg ripped a series of gashes on the steel plates below the waterline. However, *Titanic*'s bulkheads (or the walls separating the compartments in the hull) were not tall enough to contain the seawater within the damaged compartments. Surprisingly, it's been posited that if the ship had hit the iceberg head on, it may have survived with minimal damage. It has also been proposed that in a rush to complete the three ships for White Star Line, Harland and Wolff used lower-quality rivets because of a manufacturing supply issue. Had the usual, higher-quality rivets been used, the plates may have held together after the collision.

The decision to continue travel at a high speed through an area of the Atlantic commonly known as Iceberg Alley seems also to have played a part in the disaster. The initial investigations and reports from the accident confirmed that if the ship had been moving at the proper, slower speed, it would have survived the collision. However, the peaceful night and calm, glass-like ocean, along with *Titanic*'s sturdiness and air of invincibility, gave no impetus for the captain or crew to slow down.

This attitude helps explain why the failure of *Titanic* came as such a shock and provides insight into why the disaster continues to resonate today. The promise that technology would inevitably supersede humankind's limitations was the ethos of the era. Society not only experienced horror and sadness at the loss of life, it also experienced a refutation of its basic belief in the power of science and technology to overcome all human limitation and in the undisputed superiority of the educated and well-off classes. The disaster had a direct impact on naval regulations and in the adoption of new technologies for safer travel. Maritime rules in place today can be traced to the *Titanic* disaster, including lifeboat capacity requirements, availability and use of communication equipment, and warning systems such as the International Ice Patrol.

The disaster also had a nearly immediate effect on popular culture. Dozens of songs and books about the disaster came out within the year. The first film—a silent, one-reel movie starring survivor Dorothy Gibson and titled *Saved from the Titanic*—came out less than a month after the disaster.[3] Walter Lord's *A Night to Remember*, the first book considered to be a historically accurate portrayal of the complex story, was published decades later, in 1955. A 1958 British film based on the book is equally well regarded.

Despite many attempts over the years, the wreckage of the *Titanic* was not located until 1985. It took a new approach to underwater exploration developed by Robert Ballard and a breakthrough in deep-sea diving submarines to find the exact location of the ship. The discovery led to a renewed interest in the ship and an explosion of books and movies, culminating with the James Cameron Hollywood blockbuster *Titanic*. The 1997 film became an international phenomenon, broke box office records, made its two young leads superstars, and even spawned an inescapable hit song.

A hundred years after it sank, *Titanic*'s history is still being written, and its meaning continues to evolve. A company that arranges traveling expeditions controls the wreck site and most of its recovered artifacts. A major *Titanic* museum opened in Belfast in 2012, adding to the number of memorials and museums devoted to the ship's legacy. Currently, the site is designated a UNESCO (United Nations Educational, Scientific, and Cultural Organization) underwater world heritage site. *Perspectives on Modern World History: The* Titanic provides historical background on key aspects of the naval disaster; controversies about the ship, the disaster, and its legacy; and personal narratives from individuals who were directly affected by the event.

Notes

1. While precise records for the number of people on board are not available and vary slightly among different sources, there is consensus about the general distribution of passengers and survivors.
2. Cunard and White Star Line merged in 1934. The entity has been owned by Carnival Corporation since 2005. *Mauretania* held the record for fastest transatlantic crossing until 1929.
3. Unfortunately, only production stills from the movie survive. All known prints of the film were lost in a 1914 fire at the studio.

World Map

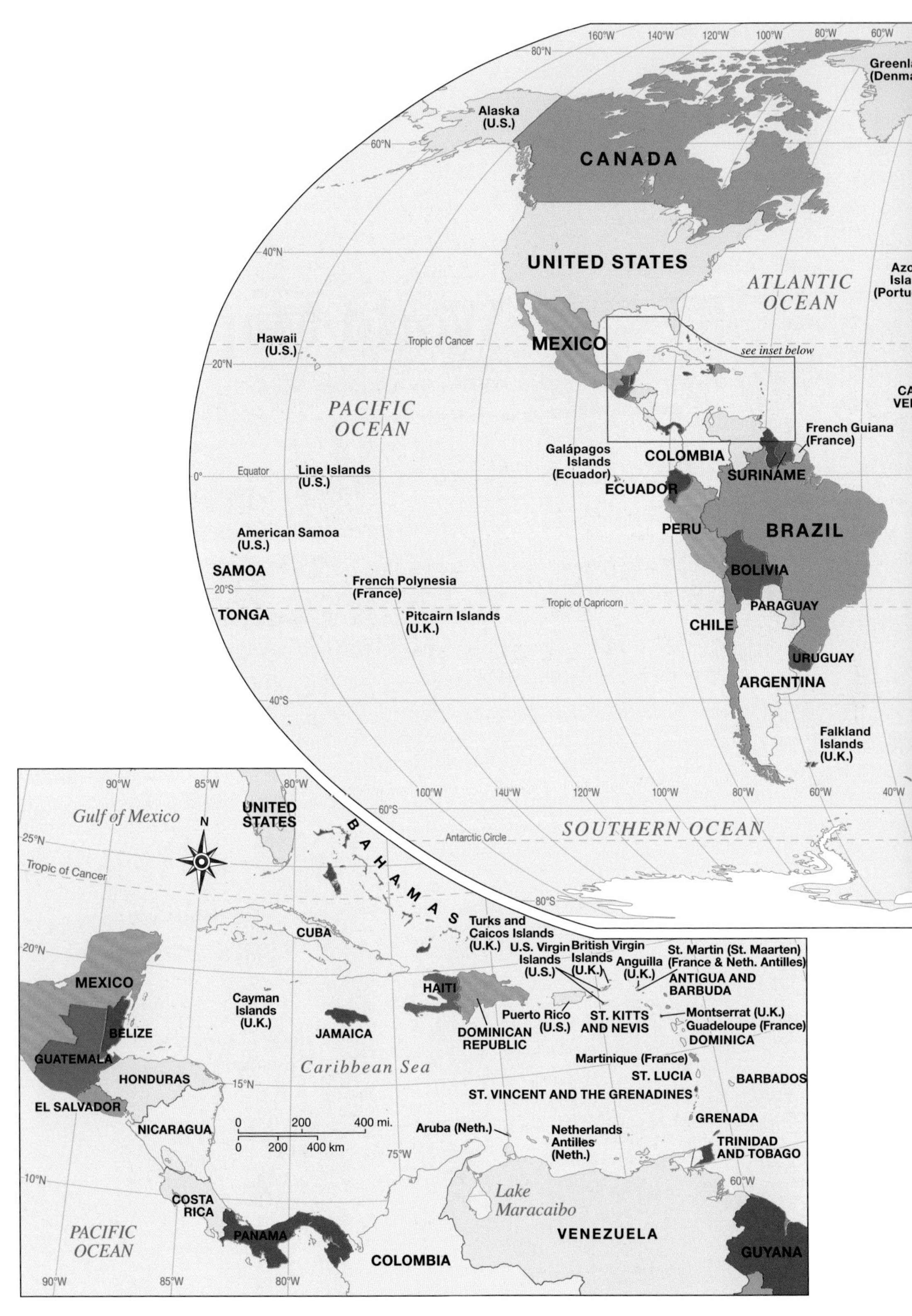

CANADA
Alaska (U.S.)
UNITED STATES
ATLANTIC OCEAN
MEXICO
Hawaii (U.S.)
Tropic of Cancer
see inset below
PACIFIC OCEAN
Galápagos Islands (Ecuador)
COLOMBIA
French Guiana (France)
SURINAME
Equator
Line Islands (U.S.)
ECUADOR
PERU
BRAZIL
American Samoa (U.S.)
SAMOA
BOLIVIA
French Polynesia (France)
TONGA
Pitcairn Islands (U.K.)
Tropic of Capricorn
PARAGUAY
CHILE
URUGUAY
ARGENTINA
Falkland Islands (U.K.)
SOUTHERN OCEAN
Antarctic Circle
Gulf of Mexico
UNITED STATES
BAHAMAS
Tropic of Cancer
Turks and Caicos Islands (U.K.)
CUBA
U.S. Virgin Islands (U.S.)
British Virgin Islands (U.K.)
Anguilla (U.K.)
St. Martin (St. Maarten) (France & Neth. Antilles)
ANTIGUA AND BARBUDA
MEXICO
HAITI
Cayman Islands (U.K.)
Puerto Rico (U.S.)
ST. KITTS AND NEVIS
Montserrat (U.K.)
Guadeloupe (France)
DOMINICA
BELIZE
JAMAICA
DOMINICAN REPUBLIC
GUATEMALA
Martinique (France)
Caribbean Sea
HONDURAS
ST. LUCIA
BARBADOS
EL SALVADOR
ST. VINCENT AND THE GRENADINES
GRENADA
NICARAGUA
Aruba (Neth.)
Netherlands Antilles (Neth.)
TRINIDAD AND TOBAGO
COSTA RICA
Lake Maracaibo
PACIFIC OCEAN
PANAMA
VENEZUELA
GUYANA
COLOMBIA

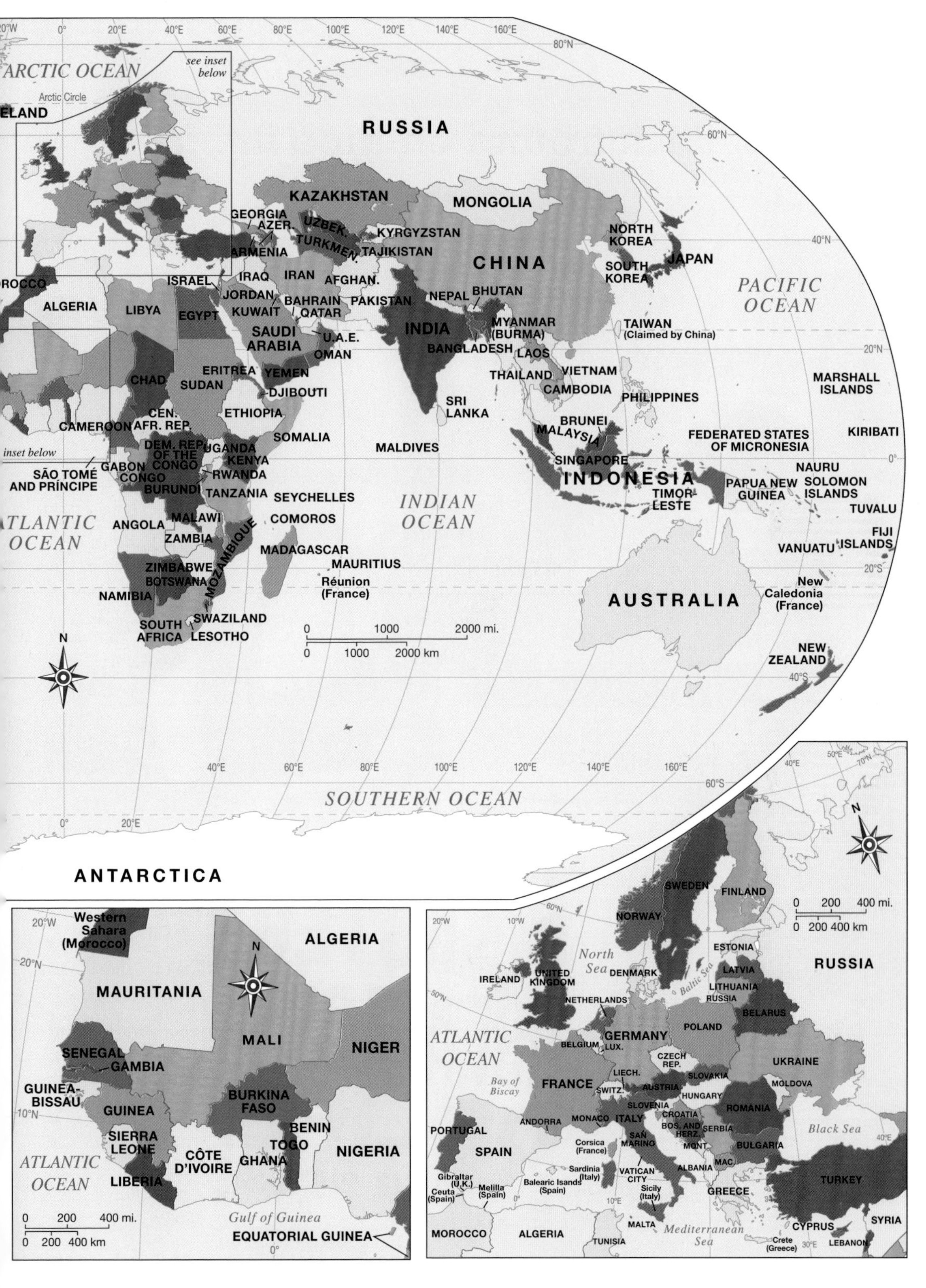

ARCTIC OCEAN
see inset below
Arctic Circle
RUSSIA
KAZAKHSTAN
MONGOLIA
GEORGIA
AZER.
UZBEK.
TURKMEN.
KYRGYZSTAN
TAJIKISTAN
ARMENIA
NORTH KOREA
SOUTH KOREA
JAPAN
CHINA
PACIFIC OCEAN
ISRAEL
IRAQ
IRAN
AFGHAN.
ALGERIA
LIBYA
EGYPT
JORDAN
KUWAIT
BAHRAIN
QATAR
PAKISTAN
NEPAL
BHUTAN
SAUDI ARABIA
U.A.E.
OMAN
INDIA
MYANMAR (BURMA)
TAIWAN (Claimed by China)
BANGLADESH
LAOS
ERITREA
YEMEN
CHAD
SUDAN
THAILAND
VIETNAM
CAMBODIA
MARSHALL ISLANDS
DJIBOUTI
PHILIPPINES
CEN. AFR. REP.
ETHIOPIA
SRI LANKA
CAMEROON
BRUNEI
MALAYSIA
SOMALIA
FEDERATED STATES OF MICRONESIA
KIRIBATI
inset below
DEM. REP. OF THE CONGO
UGANDA
KENYA
MALDIVES
SINGAPORE
SÃO TOMÉ AND PRÍNCIPE
GABON
CONGO
RWANDA
NAURU
BURUNDI
TANZANIA
INDONESIA
PAPUA NEW GUINEA
SOLOMON ISLANDS
SEYCHELLES
TIMOR-LESTE
INDIAN OCEAN
TUVALU
ATLANTIC OCEAN
ANGOLA
MALAWI
COMOROS
ZAMBIA
MOZAMBIQUE
FIJI ISLANDS
MADAGASCAR
VANUATU
ZIMBABWE
MAURITIUS
BOTSWANA
Réunion (France)
New Caledonia (France)
NAMIBIA
AUSTRALIA
SWAZILAND
SOUTH AFRICA
LESOTHO
0 1000 2000 mi.
0 1000 2000 km
NEW ZEALAND
N
SOUTHERN OCEAN
ANTARCTICA
Western Sahara (Morocco)
ALGERIA
MAURITANIA
MALI
NIGER
SENEGAL
GAMBIA
GUINEA-BISSAU
GUINEA
BURKINA FASO
BENIN
SIERRA LEONE
TOGO
CÔTE D'IVOIRE
GHANA
NIGERIA
ATLANTIC OCEAN
LIBERIA
0 200 400 mi.
0 200 400 km
Gulf of Guinea
EQUATORIAL GUINEA
SWEDEN
FINLAND
NORWAY
0 200 400 mi.
0 200 400 km
ESTONIA
North Sea
IRELAND
UNITED KINGDOM
DENMARK
LATVIA
RUSSIA
Baltic Sea
LITHUANIA
RUSSIA
NETHERLANDS
BELARUS
POLAND
ATLANTIC OCEAN
GERMANY
BELGIUM
LUX.
CZECH REP.
UKRAINE
Bay of Biscay
FRANCE
LIECH.
SLOVAKIA
SWITZ.
AUSTRIA
MOLDOVA
HUNGARY
SLOVENIA
ROMANIA
CROATIA
ANDORRA
MONACO
ITALY
BOS. AND HERZ.
SERBIA
Black Sea
PORTUGAL
SAN MARINO
BULGARIA
SPAIN
Corsica (France)
MONT.
MAC.
ALBANIA
Sardinia (Italy)
VATICAN CITY
TURKEY
Gibraltar (U.K.)
Balearic Isands (Spain)
Ceuta (Spain)
Melilla (Spain)
Sicily (Italy)
GREECE
MALTA
Mediterranean Sea
CYPRUS
SYRIA
MOROCCO
ALGERIA
TUNISIA
Crete (Greece)
LEBANON

CHAPTER 1

Historical Background on the *Titanic* Disaster

The Enduring Cultural Resonance of the *Titanic* Tragedy

Jill A. Gregg

The following viewpoint reviews the history of RMS *Titanic* and its evolution into an enduring cultural touchstone. To many contemporaries, the ship was a great symbol of human ingenuity and prowess. However, the *Titanic* disaster also illustrated the limits of technology and the growing disparity between social classes. The tragedy spurred changes in maritime law and the popularization of the wireless telegraph for naval safety. More enduring, perhaps, has been its impact on culture. The author reports that there were at least a hundred songs, a film, and books about *Titanic* within a year of the tragedy. Public interest was reawakened by the discovery of the wreckage by Robert Ballard in 1985. However, the disaster became a true cultural phenomenon after the release of the 1997 film *Titanic*, the author writes. Jill A. Gregg is an encyclopedia writer who has contributed to the *St. James Encyclopedia of Popular Culture* and

Photo on previous page: A newsboy holds a banner announcing the *Titanic* tragedy on April 15, 1912. (© **The Print Collector/Getty Images.**)

SOURCE. Jill A. Gregg, "The *Titanic*," *St. James Encyclopedia of Popular Culture*, vol. 4, pp. 661–663. Edited by Sara Pendergast and Tom Pendergast. St. James Press, 2000.

Bowling, Beatniks, and Bell-Bottoms: Pop Culture of 20th-Century America.

In the realm of popular culture, the *Titanic* has turned out to be more than just a ship that sank; it has become an icon of an era long past, as well as a contemporary phenomenon. It seems that each generation since the sinking has rediscovered the shipwreck in new books, movies, and even music.

When the luxury ocean liner *Titanic* left Queenstown, Ireland, on April 11, 1912, the ship's fame was far different than it would become in just a few short days. The voyage of the *Titanic* was a tremendous news event all around the world. The *Titanic* was the largest and most luxurious liner of its time. The world was thrilled with the improvements the industrial age had brought to their lives and *Titanic* seemed to be the ultimate realization of their dreams; many began to speak of conquering Mother Nature. When *Titanic* was called "unsinkable," some saw the description as proof of man's supremacy, while others saw it as a direct challenge to God.

Contemporaneous Responses to the Tragedy

When the *Titanic* struck an iceberg on April 14, 1912 and sank two hours later, with over 1,500 souls losing their lives, the world also lost much of its innocence and faith in man as a superior being. If this ship, so carefully planned and built to withstand anything, could sink on its maiden voyage, on what could society depend? Was the sinking a warning from God, as some religious leaders claimed? Was it meant to warn the public against the materialism of "the Gilded Age," as some proposed? Would it reverse the progress the age of industry was bringing? As is often the case with tragedies, many used the event to argue an ideological perspective. Religious

***Titanic*'s Victims and Survivors by Passenger Class**					
Passenger Category	**Percent Saved**	**Percent Lost**	**Number Saved**	**Number Lost**	**Number Aboard**
Children, First Class	100%	0%	6	0	6
Children, Second Class	100%	0%	24	0	24
Women, First Class	97%	3%	140	4	144
Women, Crew	87%	13%	20	3	23
Women, Second Class	86%	14%	80	13	93
Women, Third Class	46%	54%	76	89	165
Children, Third Class	34%	66%	27	52	79
Men, First Class	33%	67%	57	118	175
Men, Crew	22%	78%	192	693	885
Men, Third Class	16%	84%	75	387	462
Men, Second Class	8%	92%	14	154	168
Total	**32%**	**68%**	**711**	**1,513**	**2,224**

Taken from: Chuck Anesi, "The *Titanic* Casualty Figures (And What They Mean)," Anesi.com, 1997.

leaders, for example, used the example of Ida Strauss, who chose to remain with her husband on the ship, as an example to argue against divorce. Among some groups, women who survived were scolded for not following Mrs. Strauss' example and remaining with their husbands to perish. Both sides of the suffrage issue also used the *Titanic* tragedy to argue their case.

Ironically, the sinking of the *Titanic* also came to illuminate growing disparities in class around the world. In 1912, the world was marked by very distinct social classes, and it was a time when those with money were perceived as rarefied beings, somehow superior to others. Sailing on the *Titanic* were many who were of immense wealth, such as John Jacob Astor and Benjamin Guggenheim. While neither man survived, many other first class passengers did. When those numbers were compared to the number of steerage passengers rescued, an outcry was heard against the privileged. Why did they seemingly have more right to be rescued than the others? While the industrial revolution continued, there was a backlash against progress and the wealthy. Change was in the air.

> In a media-saturated society, it is only appropriate that it would not take long before the *Titanic* tragedy became a popular commodity.

The tragedy also spawned increased efforts to launch rescue operations for those involved in water accidents. In the hope of averting a repeat of the event, the International Ice Patrol was founded by the nations of the North Atlantic. The official inquiries in America and Britain also produced changes in the laws regarding lifeboats and other safety issues. After its use on the *Titanic*, the Marconi wireless apparatus [an early telegraph] was popularized to send distress signals so that rescuers on land could receive messages regarding survivors.

In a media-saturated society, it is only appropriate that it would not take long before the *Titanic* tragedy became a popular commodity. Between 1912–1913, there were at least 100 songs about the *Titanic* published, including [folk and blues musician] Leadbelly's recording of "Down with the Old Canoe." The first motion picture, starring survivor Dorothy Gibson and titled *Saved from the Titanic*, appeared just one month after the disaster and was filmed on the *Titanic*'s sister ship, the *Olympic*. Survivor Lawrence Beesley published his account, *The Loss of the S.S. Titanic*, six weeks after the tragedy. Additionally, articles appeared in *Scientific American* and other popular magazines of the time, and countless books were written surrounding the sinking. One such book, a 1898 novel by Morgan Robertson, was also rediscovered. *Futility* was the story of a ship so similar to the *Titanic* in every way, including its name, *Titan*, that many felt it had predicted the sinking of the *Titanic.*

A Resurgence of Interest

After 1913, most of the interest in the *Titanic* died down rapidly. The great ship occasionally showed up again, mainly in motion pictures, including the British film *Atlantic* (1929) and the German film *Titanic* (1943). The German film, made during World War II, was a propaganda exercise with the only heroic person on the ship a fictional German crew member. In 1953, the United States finally produced their version of the story in true Hollywood style. Starring Barbara Stanwyck and Clifton Webb, *Titanic* was a melodrama with the shipwreck used largely as a background for the fictional story of an estranged couple who reconcile as the ship sinks.

By November 1955, the *Titanic* myth experienced its first resurgence. Walter Lord, a longtime student of *Titanic* lore, published his classic—*A Night to Remember*—retelling the story of *Titanic*'s short life. By January 1956, it had sold 60,000 copies, and has never been out of print since. Another book appeared two months after Lord's, but *Down to Eternity* by Richard O'Connor was received poorly.

Not to be left out of the "picture," so to speak, in March 1956, a teleplay about the *Titanic*, directed by George Roy Hill and narrated by Claude Rains, was shown on network television. By May, an episode of the popular *You Are There* series dealt with the *Titanic.* In addition, motion pictures began appearing, including *Abandon Ship* (1957) and *A Night to Remember* (1958). The latter film, produced in documentary style, is regarded as the most faithful and accurate telling to that time. Now a permanent part of popular culture, the story

Photo on following pages: *Titanic*, the most luxurious and technologically advanced ship of its time, sank during its first voyage on April 15, 1912. More than 1,500 people died in the disaster. **(© Universal History Archive/Getty Images.)**

TITANIC

of the woman who was the most famous survivor of the *Titanic*, Margaret Tobin Brown, was chronicled in *The Unsinkable Molly Brown*. The story was first reproduced as a musical on Broadway with Tammy Grimes (1960) as the title character, and then in a motion picture with Debbie Reynolds (1964). Both were huge successes and proved there was continued interest in the shipwreck.

The *Titanic* again slipped to semi-obscurity in the mid-1960s. It did, however, remain a popular subject for the occasional television show. In 1966, the premier episode of the television adventure show, *The Time Tunnel*, dealt with the disaster. A television miniseries, *S.O.S. Titanic*, starring David Janssen as John Jacob Astor, was also produced in 1979. The ship also played an important role in fictional books such as Clive Cussler's *Raise the Titanic* (1976) and *The Memory of Eva Ryker* (1978), written by Norman Hall.

> "[Locating] the wreck of the ship . . . had long been a Holy Grail of sorts to those fascinated by it."

Robert Ballard's Discovery

On September 11, 1985, Dr. Robert Ballard of the Woods Hole Oceanographic Institute and Jean-Louis Michel of the French IFREMER Institute returned the *Titanic* to the front pages when they located the wreck of the ship. It had long been a Holy Grail of sorts to those fascinated by it, and previous expeditions had tried unsuccessfully to locate the wreckage. Dr. Ballard became an instant celebrity and a vocal critic of those who wanted to salvage items from the ship. There were even those who wanted to try to raise the *Titanic*. Articles in *National Geographic* and other magazines appeared, along with more books on the subject, including reprints of Walter Lord's book. Documentaries such as *Secrets of the Titanic* (1986) soon began to appear, and it seemed that the event was taking on a mystical quality. There was even a video game,

Search for the Titanic, appearing in 1989, that allowed players to finance and plan an expedition to locate the wreckage.

Interest remained high over the next few years as periodic new books and television specials kept the *Titanic* visible to the public. Much debate went on about whether or not to salvage any of the ship. Those who argued to salvage the ship were concerned that time was of the essence, and felt that artifacts would soon be all that was left of the event. Those against salvaging it, championed by Ballard, felt the wreck was a memorial and should be left alone. Eventually, the pro-salvage group won, and artifacts from the ship were eventually brought to the surface.

"Nothing . . . could prepare the world for the coming of the James Cameron film."

On April 23, 1997, a new interpretation of the disaster appeared when *Titanic: A New Musical*—a big budget theater production—debuted on Broadway. In a theater season with few successes and even fewer legitimate hits, this musical was the smash of the season; it won 5 Tony awards, including one for Best Musical.

James Cameron's Blockbuster

Nothing, however, could prepare the world for the coming of the James Cameron film, *Titanic*, in 1997. Amid rumor and innuendo regarding "the most expensive film ever made," the public waited for its release and a chance to it judge for themselves. When the release date was delayed and the film went over budget, many predicted another disaster, this one of a business nature. Would it be a hit or the most expensive miss in motion picture history? It became obvious after the film's initial release that Cameron did not need to worry. *Titanic* became the largest grossing movie ever and tied previous Academy Award winner *Ben Hur* (1959) for most trophies won, with 11. The soundtrack from the movie became the best selling movie soundtrack in history; the love theme from the movie, "My Heart Will Go On," performed by Celine Dion, quickly became a number one song. And the stars of the motion picture, Leonardo DiCaprio and Kate Winslet, both relatively unknown before the film, became superstars.

The public could not get enough of the film or the ship. Using life-size models and computer generated images, the film was generally considered the most historically accurate, although some historians disagreed with liberties taken with some of the characters in the film. The Edwardian hairstyles and wardrobe depicted sparked a fashion craze, and the blue diamond necklace that was a centerpiece of the plot became a best selling piece of costume jewelry.

A Cultural Phenomenon

In the late twentieth century, the *Titanic* continues to fascinate the public. There are faithful *Titanic* buffs who have read about and pondered the fate of the vessel for many years. Many of them are members of the Titanic Historical Society, whose headquarters are in a jewelry store in Indian Orchard, Massachusetts. Membership increases every time the *Titanic* returns to the front page of the news, but it took a blockbuster film to make the *Titanic* a true cultural phenomenon among the general public. The *Titanic* remains a commodity to be bought and sold. The sinking of the *Titanic* is a historic tragedy which will forever be a part of history and of popular culture.

How the World's Greatest Steamship Went Down

Scientific American

In a viewpoint originally published just weeks after the *Titanic* tragedy, the editors of a popular science magazine review the known facts and describe the ship's sinking as a wholly preventable accident. The authors detail *Titanic*'s design and construction, including the novel safety features that should have prevented it from sinking. They explain that the iceberg collision had a lethal effect primarily because of the ship's speed, which was unusually fast for traveling through a known ice field. Furthermore, choices made by the ship's designers that limited lifeboat capacity were negligent and resulted in unnecessary loss of life. Founded in 1845, *Scientific American* is the oldest continuously published magazine in the United States. It is known for presenting scientific concepts in clear and informative formats to the general audience.

SOURCE. "Wreck of the White Star Liner *Titanic*," *Scientific American*, vol. 106, no. 17, pp. 380–381. April 27, 2012. Reproduced by permission

In the long list of maritime disasters there is none to compare with that which, on Sunday, April 14th [1912], overwhelmed the latest and most magnificent of the ocean liners on her maiden voyage across the Western Ocean. Look at the disaster from whatever point we may, it stands out stupefying in its horror and prodigious in its many-sided significance.

The Last Word in Naval Architecture

The *Titanic* stood for the "last word" in naval architecture. Not only did she carry to a far greater degree than any other ship the assurance of safety which we have come to associate with mere size; not only did she embody every safeguard against accident, known to the naval architect; not only was there wrought into her structure a greater proportionate mass of steel than had been put into any, even of the recent giant liners; but she was built at the foremost shipyard of Great Britain, and by a company whose vessels are credited with being the most strongly and carefully constructed of any afloat.

To begin with, the floor of the ship was of exceptional strength and stiffness. Keel, keelson, longitudinals and inner and outer bottoms, were of a weight, size and thickness exceeding those of any previous ship. The floor was carried well up into the sides of the vessel, and in addition to the conventional framing, the hull was stiffened by deep web frames—girders of great strength—spaced at frequent and regular intervals throughout the whole length of the vessel. Tying the ship's sides together were the deck beams, 10 inches in depth, covered, floor above floor, with unbroken decks of steel. Additional strength was afforded by the stout longitudinal bulkheads of the coal bunkers, which extended in the wake of the boiler rooms, and, incidentally, by their watertight construction, served, or rather, in view of the loss of the ship, we should say were intended to serve, to prevent water,

A photograph from May 1911 shows *Titanic* under construction at the Harland and Wolff shipyard in Belfast, Ireland. (© Popperfoto/ Getty Images.)

which might enter through a rupture in the ship's outer shell, from finding its way into the boiler rooms.

As a further protection against sinking, the *Titanic* was divided by 15 transverse bulkheads into 16 separate watertight compartments; and they were so proportioned that any two of them might have been flooded without endangering the flotation of the ship. Furthermore, all the multitudinous compartments of the cellular double bottom, and all the 16 main compartments of the ship, were connected through an elaborate system of piping, with a series of powerful pumps, whose joint capacity would suffice to greatly delay the rise of water in the holds, due to any of the ordinary accidents of the sea involving a rupture of the hull of the ship.

Size as an Element of Safety

Finally there was the security against foundering due to vast size—a safeguard which might reasonably be considered the most effective of all. For it is certain that with a given amount of damage to the hull, the flooding of one compartment will affect the stability of a ship in the inverse ratio of her size—or, should the water-tight doors fail to close, the ship will stay afloat for a length of time approximately proportional to her size.

> She [*Titanic*] could have taken the blow of a colliding ship on bow, quarter or abeam and remained afloat.

And so, for many and good reasons, the ship's company who set sail from Southampton [England] on the first and last voyage of the world's greatest vessel believed that she was unsinkable.

And unsinkable she was by any of the seemingly possible accidents of wind and weather or deep-sea collision. She could have taken the blow of a colliding ship on bow, quarter or abeam and remained afloat, or even made her way to port. *Bow on, and under the half speed called on by careful seamanship*, she could probably have come without fatal injury through the ordeal of head-on collision with an iceberg.

But there was just one peril of the deep against which this mighty ship was as helpless as the smallest of coasting steamers—the long, glancing blow below the waterline, due to the projecting shelf of an iceberg. It was this that sent the *Titanic* to the bottom in the brief space of 2½ hours, and it was her very size and the fatal speed at which she was driven, which made the blow so terrible. . . . The indicated horsepower of the *Titanic* was 50,000, developed in two reciprocating engines driving two wing propellers and a single turbine driving a central propeller. The ship had accommodations for a whole townful of people (3,356, as a matter of fact), of whom 750 could be accommodated in the first class,

550 in the second, and 1,200 in the third. The balance of the company was made up of 63 officers and sailors, 322 engineers, firemen, oilers, and 471 stewards, waiters, etc.

Taking a Chance Through the Ice Field

When the *Titanic* left Southampton on her fatal voyage she had on board a total of 2,340 passengers and crew. The voyage was uneventful until Sunday, April 14th, when the wireless operator received and acknowledged a message from the *Amerika*, warning her of the existence of a large field of ice into which her course would lead her toward the close of the day.

The *Titanic* had been running at a steady speed of nearly 22 knots, having covered 545 miles during the day ending at noon April 14th; yet, in spite of the grave danger presented by the ice field ahead, she seems to have maintained during Sunday night a speed of not less than 21 knots. This is made clear by the testimony of Mr. [J. Bruce] Ismay, of the White Star Line, who stated at the Senate investigation that the revolutions were 72 as against the 78 revolutions which gave her full speed. She could make about 22½ knots at full speed, and 72 revolutions would correspond to about 21 knots.

How such an experienced commander as Captain [Edward] Smith should have driven his ship at high speed, and in the night, when he knew that he was in the proximity of heavy ice fields is a mystery which may never be cleared up. The night, it is true, was clear and starlit, and the sea perfectly smooth. Probably the fact that conditions were favorable for a good lookout, coupled with the desire to maintain a high average speed on the maiden trip of the vessel, decided the captain to "take a chance." Whatever the motive, it seems to be well established that the ship was not slowed down; and to this fact and no other must the loss of the *Titanic* be set down.

Had the *Titanic* been running under a slow bell, she would probably have been afloat today.

The Fatal Blow

There were the usual lookout men at the bow and in the crow's nest, and officers on the bridge were straining their eyes for indications of the dreaded ice, when the cry suddenly rang out from the crow's nest, "Berg ahead," and an iceberg loomed up in the ship's path, distant only a quarter of a mile. The first officer gave the order "Starboard your helm." The great ship answered smartly and swung swiftly to port. But it was too late. The vessel took the blow of a deadly, underwater, projecting shelf of ice, on her starboard bow near the bridge, and before she swung clear, the mighty ram of the iceberg had torn its way through plating and frames as far aft as amidships, opening up compartment after compartment to the sea.

> There is remarkable unanimity of testimony on the part of the survivors as to the slight nature of the [collision].

Thus, at one blow, were all the safety appliances of this magnificent ship set at naught! Of what avail was it to close water-tight doors, or set going the powerful pumps, when nearly half the length of the ship was open to the inpouring water. It must have taken but a few minutes' inspection to show the officers of the ship that she was doomed. . . . But had the speed been only one-half and the energy one-fourth as great, the ship might well have been deflected from the iceberg before more than two or three of her compartments had been ripped open; and with the water confined to these, the powerful pumps could have kept the vessel afloat for many hours, and surely until a fleet of rescuing ships had taken every soul from the stricken vessel.

There is remarkable unanimity of testimony on the part of the survivors as to the slight nature of the shock; and this, coupled with the universal confidence in the unsinkability of the vessel, and the perfect quiet of both sea and ship, contributed no doubt to the marvelous absence of panic among the passengers.

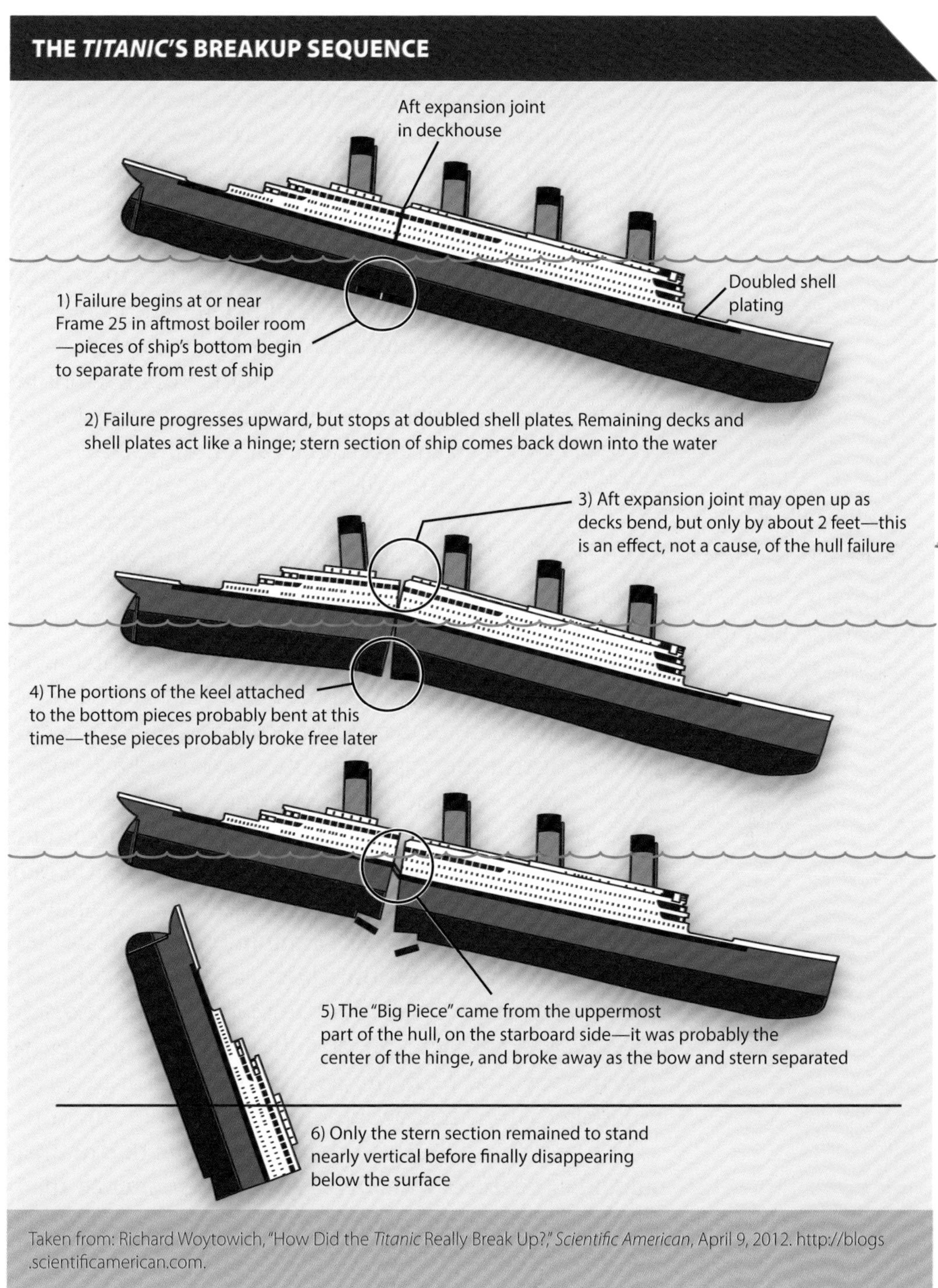

Taken from: Richard Woytowich, "How Did the *Titanic* Really Break Up?," *Scientific American*, April 9, 2012. http://blogs.scientificamerican.com.

The Criminal Lack of Lifeboats

The wireless again, as in the case of the *Republic* [collision in 1909], proved its inestimable value. The collision occurred at 11:40 Sunday night in latitude 41.16 north, longitude 50.14 west. The call for help was heard by several ships, the nearest of which was the *Carpathia*, which caught the message at 12:35 AM Monday, when she was 58 miles distant from the *Titanic*. Setting an extra watch the captain crowded on all speed, reaching the scene of the disaster by 4 AM.

> We can conceive of no other motive than . . . commercial expediency . . . for this criminal reduction [of lifeboats].

Meanwhile, with the ship sinking swiftly beneath them, there remained as a last hope for that hapless multitude the boats. The boats! Twenty in all, with a maximum accommodation of say 1,000 for 2,340 human beings!

For years the British Board of Trade, renowned the world over for the jealous care with which it safeguards the life of the individual, has been guilty of the amazing anomaly of permitting the passenger ships of the vast British merchant marine to put to sea carrying boat accommodation for only one out of every three persons on board. The penalty for such unspeakable folly, we had almost said criminal and brutal negligence, may have been long delayed; but it was to come this night in a wholesale flinging away of human life, which has left a blot upon this institution which can never be effaced! Had the regulations called for the boat accommodation demanded by the German or our own government, every soul on board the *Titanic* could have been transferred and picked up by the rescuing ship.

We can conceive of no other motive than that of commercial expediency, the desire to reserve valuable space for restaurants, sun parlors or other superfluous but attractive features of the advertising pamphlet and the placard, for this criminal reduction of the last recourse of the shipwrecked to so small a measure.

No practical steamship man can claim that the provision of boat accommodation for the full complement of a ship like the *Titanic* was impracticable. The removal of deckhouse structures from the boat deck of the ship, and the surrender of this deck to its proper uses, would give ample storage room for the sixty boats, more or less, which would be necessary. . . .

How the Great Ship Went Down

Piecing together what the survivors witnessed from the boats, it is easy to understand the successive events of the ship's final plunge. The filling of the forward compartments brought her down by the head, and, gradually, to an almost vertical position. Here she hung a while, stern high in air, like a huge, weighted spar buoy. As she swung to the perpendicular, her heavy engines and boilers, tearing loose from their foundations, crashed forward (downward); and, the water pressure increasing as the sank, burst in the so far intact after compartments. It was the muffled roar of this "death rattle" of the dying ship that caused some survivors to tell of bursting boilers and a hull broken apart. The shell of the ship, except for the injuries received in the collision, went to the bottom intact. When the after compartments finally gave way, the stricken vessel, weighted with the mass of engine and boiler-room wreckage at her forward end, sank, to bury herself, bows down, in the soft ooze of the Atlantic bottom, two miles below. There, for aught we know, she may at this moment be standing, with several hundred feet of her rising sheer above the ocean floor, a sublime memorial shaft to the sixteen hundred hapless souls who perished in this unspeakable tragedy!

Titanic Sends Its Final Wireless Messages

Great Yarmouth Radio Club

The messages sent and received by *Titanic* the night of April 14–15, 1912, have been transcribed and reproduced in the following viewpoint. While the original radio log went down with the ship, the transcripts were re-created by the Marconi Corporation for use during investigations into the disaster. (Marconi developed and installed the wireless telegraph used by *Titanic* and employed the vast majority of seagoing radio officers at the time.) The viewpoint also includes notes and clarifications about the events surrounding the transmissions. The frantic tone of the communications between *Titanic* and a number of ships over a wide area of the North Atlantic is vividly captured in the transcripts. The Great Yarmouth Radio Club is a nearly hundred-year-old association of amateur radio enthusiasts in Norfolk, England.

SOURCE. Nigel Brown, "The Final Wireless Transmission Aboard the *Titanic*," Great Yarmouth Radio Club, n.d. (1912).

Manned by John George Phillips and Harold Bride, the *Titanic*'s wireless room had been doing steady business since the ship had left port. The machine went down on Saturday evening, April 13th, and had not been repaired until nearly 5.00 AM, Sunday, April 14th.

Prior to April 14th, 1912, the *Titanic* had received several ice warnings, from the ships *Caronia*, *La Touraine*, *Amerika*, and *Rappahannock*. The message from the *Caronia* had been posted in the officer's chart room. Wireless operator Harold Bride shut down the telegraph for a while on April 14th, 1912 to let the machine cool, and missed an ice warning from the *Californian*.

While these are not every wireless message to go from or to the *Titanic*, they are the most pertinent to the tragedy which befell the ship.

Ice Warnings

1.40 PM, 14 April 1912, S.S. *Baltic* to R.M.S. *Titanic*. "Captain Smith, *Titanic*. Have had moderate variable winds and clear fine weather since leaving. Greek steamer *Athinai* reports passing icebergs and large quantity of field ice today in latitude 41.51 N, longitude 49.52 W. Last night we spoke (with) German oil tanker *Deutschland*, Stettin to Philadelphia, not under control, short of coal; latitude 40.42 N, longitude 55.11 W. Wishes to be reported to New York and other steamers. Wish you and *Titanic* all success".

7.30 PM, 14 April 1912, S.S. *Antillian* to R.M.S. *Titanic*. "6.30 PM, apparent time, ship; latitude 42.3 N, longitude 49.9 W. Three large bergs five mile to southward of us".

9.30 PM, 14 April 1912, S.S. *Mesaba* to R.M.S. *Titanic* and All Eastbound Ships. "Ice report. In latitude 42 N to 41.25 N, longitude 49 W to 50.3 W. Saw much heavy pack ice and great number of large icebergs, also field ice. Weather good, clear".

9.35 PM, 14 April 1912, R.M.S. *Titanic* to S.S. *Mesaba*. "Received, thanks".

9.38 PM, 14 April 1912, S.S. *Mesaba* to R.M.S. *Titanic*. "Stand by". (Stanley Adams, on the S.S. *Mesaba*, was waiting for the *Titanic* to indicate the message had been given to the captain. Jack Phillips did not respond, but continued to send passenger messages to Cape Race.)

11.00 PM (approx), 14 April 1912, R.M.S. *Californian* to R.M.S. *Titanic*. "Say, old man, we are stopped and surrounded by ice".

11.10 PM (approx), 14 April 1912, R.M.S. *Titanic* to R.M.S. *Californian*. Keep out! Shut up, shut up! I am busy, I am working Cape Race.

11.15 P.M. (approx), 14 April 1912, R.M.S. *Titanic* to Cape Race, Newfoundland. "Sorry, please repeat. Jammed".

Initial Distress Calls

Between 11.35 and 11.45 PM (most likely the latter) Captain [Edward] Smith informed Phillips and Bride that the ship had hit an iceberg, and to prepare a distress call. The captain returned at 12.15 AM and told them to send it.

12.15 AM, 15 April 1912, R.M.S. *Titanic* to Any Ship. "CQD *Titanic* 41.44 N 50.24 W". (CQD was the contemporary distress signal, though soon, the new distress signal would be put to use for the very first time).

12.17 AM, 15 April 1912, R.M.S. *Titanic* to Any Ship. "CQD CQD SOS *Titanic* Position 41.44 N 50.24 W. Require immediate assistance. Come at once. We struck an iceberg.

Sinking". (SOS was the first use of the new distress signal. So far, two ships had responded to the *Titanic*'s distress call. They included the *Frankfurt*, nearly 170 miles away, and the *Olympic*, nearly 500 miles away.)

12.20 AM, 15 April 1912, R.M.S. *Titanic* to R.M.S. *Carpathia*. "Come at once. We have struck a berg. It's a CQD, old man. Position 41.46 N 50.14 W".

12.21 AM, 15 April 1912, R.M.S. *Carpathia* to R.M.S. *Titanic*. "I say old man, do you know there is a batch of messages coming through for you from MCC (MCC indicated Cape Cod)?"

12.22 AM, 15 April 1912, R.M.S. *Titanic* to R.M.S. *Carpathia*. "CQD CQD".

12.25 AM, 15 April 1912, R.M.S. *Carpathia* to R.M.S. *Titanic*. "Shall I tell my captain? Do you require assistance?"

12.26 AM, 15 April 1912, R.M.S. *Titanic* to R.M.S. *Carpathia*. "Yes, come quick!"

12.32 AM, 15 April 1912, R.M.S. *Carpathia* to R.M.S. *Titanic*. "Putting about and heading for you".

12.40 AM, 15 April 1912, R.M.S. *Titanic* to R.M.S. *Carpathia*. "SOS *Titanic* sinking by the head. We are about all down. Sinking . . ."

From 12.40 AM until the final message was sent from the *Titanic* sometime between 2.15 AM and 2.25 AM the *Titanic*, the *Carpathia* and other ships kept a steady stream of messages, updating their progress and *Titanic*'s condition. The *Titanic* continued to send out general CQD and SOS messages, in the chance that there might be a closer ship.

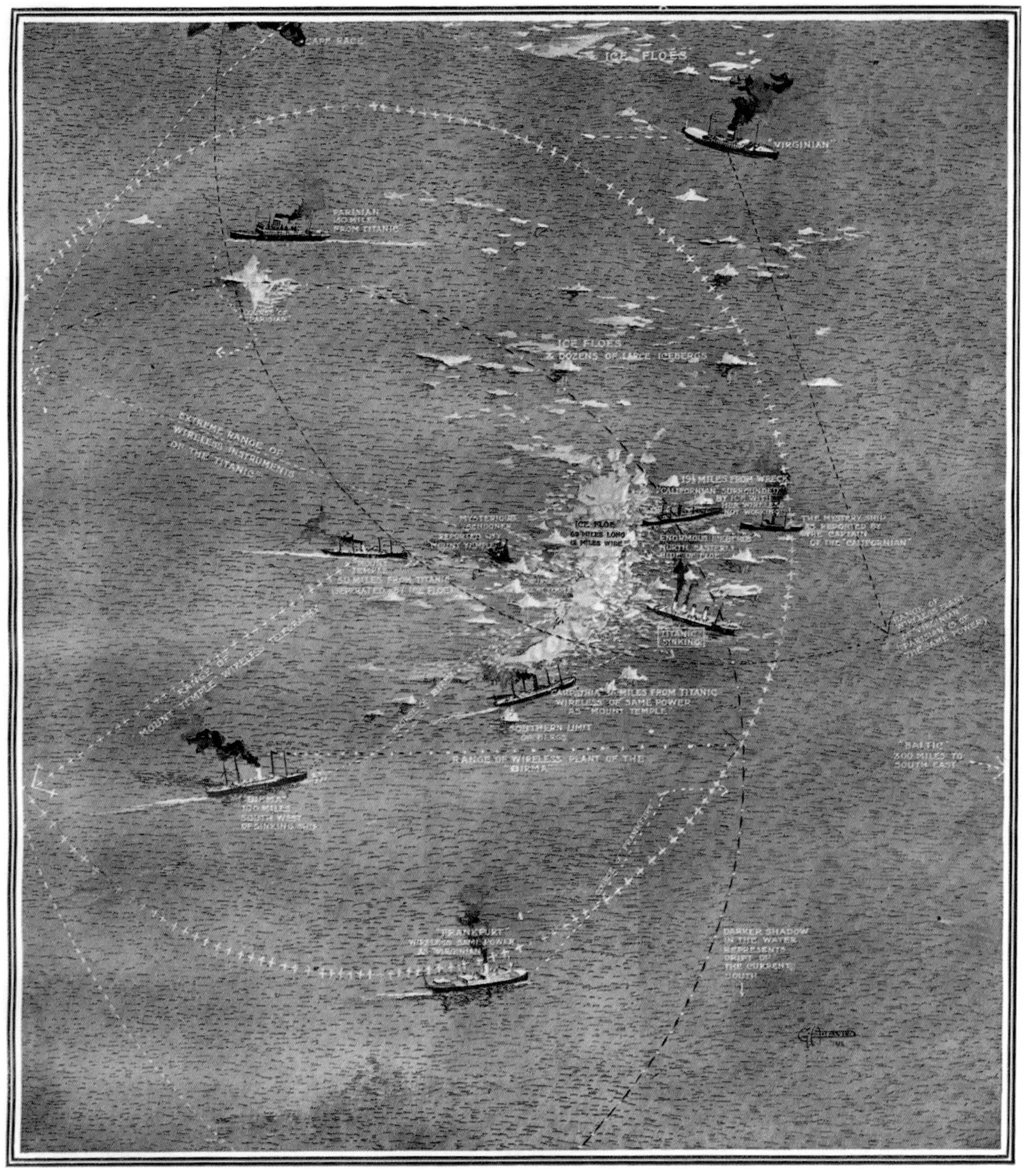

Communications with *Olympic*

12.45 AM, 15 April 1912. *Titanic* calls *Olympic*, (sister ship —500 miles away en route to England) "SOS". (First use of SOS by *Titanic*. Bride jokingly suggests to Phillips that it may be his last chance to use the new distress call.)

12.50 AM, 15 April 1912. *Titanic* calls CQD and says, "I require immediate assistance. Position 41.46 N. 50.14 W." Received by *Celtic.*

Photo on opposite page: A 1912 illustration shows the approximate positions of ships on the northern Atlantic Ocean during the sinking of *Titanic*. (© **Universal Images Group/Getty Images.**)

12.53 AM, 15 April 1912, *Caronia* to MBC (*Baltic*). MGY (*Titanic*) CQD in 41.46 N. 40.14 W. Wants immediate assistance".

1.00 AM, 15 April 1912. MGY (*Titanic*) gives distress signal. DDC (*Cincinnati*) replies. MGY's (*Titanic*) position 41.46 N. 50.14 W. Assistance from DDC (*Cincinnati*) not necessary as MKC (*Olympic*) shortly afterwards answers distress call.

1.00 AM, 15 April 1912. *Titanic* replies to *Olympic* and gives her position as 41.46 N. 50.14 W., and says, "We have struck an iceberg".

1.02 AM, 15 April 1912. *Titanic* calls *Asian* and said, "Want immediate assistance". *Asian* answered at once and received *Titanic*'s position as 41.46 N. 50.14 W., which was immediately taken to the bridge. Captain Smith instructs operator to have *Titanic*'s position repeated.

1.02 AM, 15 April 1912. *Virginian* calls *Titanic* but gets no response. Cape Race tells *Virginian* to report to his Captain that the *Titanic* has struck iceberg and requires immediate assistance.

1.10 AM, 15 April 1912, *Titanic* to MKC (*Olympic*). "We are in collision with berg. Sinking Head down. 41.46 N. 50.14 W. Come soon as possible".

1.10 AM, 15 April 1912, *Titanic* to MKC (*Olympic*). Captain says, "Get your boats ready. What is your position?"

Other Ships Rush to Help

1.15 AM, 15 April 1912, *Baltic* to *Caronia*. "Please tell *Titanic* we are making towards her".

1.20 AM, 15 April 1912. *Virginian* hears MCE (Cape Race) inform MGY (*Titanic*) "That we are going to her assistance. Our position 170 miles N. of *Titanic*".

1.25 A.M., 15 April 1912, *Caronia* to *Titanic*. "*Baltic* coming to your assistance".

1.27 AM, 15 April 1912. *Olympic* sends position to *Titanic*, "1.24 AM G.M.T. 40.52 N. 61.18 W", and asks "Are you steering southerly to meet us?" *Titanic* replies, "We are putting the women off in the boats".

1.30 AM, 15 April 1912. *Titanic* to *Olympic*. "We are putting passengers off in small boats." "Women and children in boats, cannot last much longer".

1.35 AM, 15 April 1912. *Olympic* asks *Titanic* what weather she had. *Titanic* replies, "Clear and calm".

1.35 AM, 15 April 1912. *Baltic* hears *Titanic* say, "Engine room getting flooded." (Captain Smith had just visited the *Titanic*'s radio room and advised this to Phillips and Bride).

1.35 AM, 15 April 1912. *Mount Temple* hears DFT (*Frankfurt*) ask, "Are there any boats around you already?" No reply.

1.37 AM, 15 April 1912, *Baltic* to *Titanic*. "We are rushing to you".

1.40 AM, 15 April 1912, *Olympic* to *Titanic*. "Am lighting up all possible boilers as fast as (we) can".

Wireless Ship Act Amendment of 1912

In July 1912, as a result of the Titanic *disaster, the US law requiring apparatus and operators for radio communication on ocean steamers was amended to read as follows:*

From and after October first, nineteen hundred and twelve, it shall be unlawful for any steamer of the United States or of any foreign country navigating the ocean or the Great Lakes and licensed to carry, or carrying, fifty or more persons, including passengers or crew or both, to leave or attempt to leave any port of the United States unless such steamer shall be equipped with an efficient apparatus for radio communication, in good working order, capable of transmitting and receiving messages over a distance of at least one hundred miles, day or night. An auxiliary power supply, independent of the vessel's main electric power plant, must be provided which will enable the sending set for at least four hours to send messages over a distance of at least one hundred miles, day or night, and efficient communication between the operator in the radio room and the bridge shall be maintained at all times.

The radio equipment must be in charge of two or more persons skilled in the use of such apparatus, one or the other of whom shall be on duty at all times while the vessel is being navigated. Such equipment, operators, the regulation of their watches, and the transmission and receipt of messages, except as may be regulated by law or international agreement, shall be under the control of the master, in the case of a vessel of the United States; and every willful failure on the part of the master to enforce at sea the provisions of this paragraph as to equipment, operators, and watches shall subject him to a penalty of one hundred dollars.

The provisions of this section shall not apply to steamers plying between ports, or places, less than two hundred miles apart.

SOURCE. *US Department of Commerce, "Part XXXVIII: Radio Communication,"* Navigation Laws of the United States. *Washington, DC: Government Printing Office, 1919.*

1.40 AM, 15 April 1912, Cape Race to *Virginia*. "Please tell your Captain this. The *Olympic* is making all speed for *Titanic*, but her (*Olympic*'s) position is 40.32 N. 61.18 W.

You are much nearer to *Titanic*. The *Titanic* is already putting women off in the boats, and she says the weather there is calm and clear. The *Olympic* is the only ship we have heard say, 'Going to the assistance of the *Titanic*.' The others must be a long way from the *Titanic*".

Lost Connection with *Titanic*

1.45 AM, 15 April 1912. Last signals heard from *Titanic* by *Carpathia*, "Come as quickly as possible old man. our engine-room is filling up to the boilers".

1.45 AM, 15 April 1912. *Mount Temple* hears *Frankfurt* calling *Titanic*. No reply.

1.47 AM, 15 April 1912. *Caronia* hears *Titanic* though signals unreadable still.

1.48 AM, 15 April 1912. *Asian* heard *Titanic* call SOS. *Asian* answers *Titanic* but receives no answer.

DFT (*Frankfurt*) calls *Titanic* and says, "What is the matter with u?"

1.50 AM, 15 April 1912, Titanic to *Frankfurt*. "You are a fool, stdbi—stdbi—stdbi and keep out".

Caronia hears *Frankfurt* working to *Titanic*. *Frankfurt* according to position 172 miles from MGY (*Titanic*) at time first SOS sent out.

1.55 AM, 15 April 1912, Cape Race to *Virginian*. "We have not heard *Titanic* for about half an hour. Her power may be gone".

2.00 AM, 15 April 1912. *Virginian* hears *Titanic* calling very faintly, her power being greatly reduced.

2.10 AM, 15 April 1912. *Virginian* hears 2 V's signalled faintly in spark similar to *Titanic*'s (Phillips adjusting his transmitter to compensate for the dying power supply from the engine room).

2.17 AM, 15 April 1912. *Virginian* hears *Titanic*, call "CQ" (call to all ships), but unable to read him. *Titanic*'s signals end very abruptly as power suddenly switched off. (Phillips had actually intended to send "CQD DE MGY", however at this point there is a loss of all power to the radio room—water can be heard flooding the wheelhouse—Phillips says to Bride "Come on, let's clear out". Bride climbs to the roof of the officer's quarters and assists with launching collapsible Lifeboat B—Phillips disappears aft).

The Final Wireless Message

Sometime between 2.15 AM and 2.25 AM, 15 April 1912, R.M.S. *Titanic* to R.M.S. *Carpathia*. "SOS SOS CQD CQD *Titanic*. We are sinking fast. Passengers are being put into boats. *Titanic*."

Bride and Phillips left the wireless room after that message, after being urged to leave their post by Captain Smith. They made their way to the Boat-Deck and began trying to help the other men in the releasing of collapsible Lifeboat B. While neither of them immediately made it onto a lifeboat, both were rescued from the sea. Bride's feet were so severely frozen he could not walk. Phillips died of hypothermia on or near collapsible Lifeboat B, his body was never recovered.

VIEWPOINT 4

Confusion Reigns as News of the Disaster Reaches New York

New York Times

The following viewpoint reports on the chaos of information and misinformation during the four days between the sinking of *Titanic* and the arrival of survivors in New York City. The author describes the scene as several thousand people gather in the streets to read bulletins posted on the headquarters building of the *New York Times*. Friends and family of *Titanic* passengers are told repeatedly by White Star Line officials that there was no loss of life, the author reports. However, the author also explains that staff at the company had received few messages or clear information themselves. Through it all, the notion that *Titanic* was unsinkable continues, even in reports about the rescue at sea. RMS *Carpathia* reached New York carrying only 705 *Titanic* survivors two days after this viewpoint was originally published. The *New York Times* has been published since 1851 and is generally regarded as the national paper of record.

SOURCE. "Women Sob as News Bulletins Appear; Thousands Stand in Times Square Till Midnight to Learn Details of Disaster," *New York Times*, April 15, 1912. Reproduced by permission.

The bulletins posted in quick succession from 7:30 to 10 o'clock, and at slightly longer intervals thereafter, proved a profound surprise to thousands who congregated in Times Square.

People rushing along the street at 7:30 o'clock carried final editions of the evening papers declaring that all were saved, and that the *Titanic* was under tow en route to Halifax. Some of them stopped as if transfixed as they caught sight of the bulletin declaring the *Titanic* had gone down and all on board except the women and children had been lost.

From about 100 watchers who had been following the earlier bulletins the crowd in Times Square sprang within fifteen minutes to something over 4,000. A cleared space ten feet in width was maintained on the sidewalk adjoining the Times Building, but Broadway, on the east side of the building, was packed as far as the street car tracks, while on the north the crowd stretched far out into the automobile stand maintained north of Forty-third Street.

Many on their way home from business attempted to hurry past in the cleared space on Broadway, close to the bulletin board. They glanced hurriedly at the bulletins and lingered as if unable to comprehend the meaning. At the first place they could stop after leaving the main traffic channel they did so, and then stood for hours, as the fresh dispatches continued to hold them fascinated.

Displays of New Technology and Public Grief

With the synchronized bulletin machines flashing the news to immense throngs north and east of the Time Building on three separate bulletin boards, and to another throng far downtown from another bulletin board, all operated from a single centre, the spectators realized that they were receiving news of an overwhelming event in a manner that only a little time ago was unthought of.

Conversations, sometimes half hysterical, sometimes filled with sobbing, were heard on every side. Many women, when asked why they were crying, said they had no relatives aboard and no reason to sob except that the bulletins overcame them.

Above the hum of conversation occasional phrases were caught indicating the tense strain which everyone felt. Here are a few exclamations heard:

> The whole bottom must have been torn open.
>
> I do hope it isn't true.
>
> How could it happen? I hope someone responsible who can tell all about it, was saved.
>
> Could the ship have broken in two?
>
> The *Titanic* must have been going at a terrific speed.

Two men and a woman came to the bulletin board together and crowded close to the front of the throng. The woman screamed as she read the bulletins and the men brought her inside the Times Building. One of the men said the woman was his sister and that relatives were aboard the *Titanic*. The man remained calm for a few minutes, then, rushing to William J. Mass, who was printing *The Times* bulletins on the machine that was sending them to all the bulletin boards simultaneously, he shouted:

> 'How dare you say [*Titanic*'s passengers are] all lost now, when they were saying all day they were all saved?'

> How dare you—how dare you say they're all lost now when they were saying all day they were all saved? How dare you do it?

Refusing to give his name, he seized the woman by the arm and led her back into the crowd.

The White Star Line's Encouraging Messages

The crowds of men and women who had friends on the *Titanic* and who kept drifting all day yesterday into the White Star offices from the opening of the office early in the morning received positive assurances. The officers of the line who answered inquiries said that the sinking of the largest vessel afloat, with her many devices for safety, was an utter impossibility. There had been no loss of life, these men and women were told again and again. Reports showed that even if the vessel was "down by the head," her passengers were being taken off in safely.

"How could she sink with those fifteen bulkheads and her many water-tight compartments," was repeated again and again. The officers of the line admitted that they were rather uncertain as to facts, that messages had been few, and that these simply repeated what was known through press messages, and all were encouraging in character. The first message given out by P.A.S. Franklin, Vice President of the International Mercantile Marine Company, was headed "No Alarm for *Titanic*'s Passengers." It follows:

> P.A.S. Franklin, Vice President of the International Mercantile Marine Company, said this morning that while no direct message from the *Titanic* had been received at the office, the officials were perfectly satisfied that there was no cause for alarm regarding the safety of the passengers of the ship, as they regard the *Titanic* as being practically unsinkable. They do not regard the cessation of the ship's wireless messages as denoting anything serious, as this might have been caused by atmospheric disturbances or other causes. The *Titanic* is well able to withstand almost any exterior damage and could keep afloat indefinitely after being struck.
>
> The *Titanic* is now in latitude 41.66 north and longitude 50.14 west. She is being approached from the

> west by the *Olympic* of the White Star Line, which, they figure, will be alongside by 8 PM to-day. The *Baltic* of the same line, which was east of the *Titanic* on its way to Europe, has turned back and will probably be alongside the *Titanic* by 4 PM to-day. The *Virginian* of the Allen Line, eastward bound, is reported as rapidly approaching, and should be on the spot by 10 o'clock this morning.
>
> The *Olympic* has just been reported as having been in direct communication by wireless with the *Titanic*.
>
> Mr. Franklin was most emphatic in the assurances regarding the safety of the passengers and the steamer.

Mr. Franklin added to this statement by repeating that he did not attach any significance to the fact that there were not Marconi messages being received from the *Titanic*. That, he said, denoted nothing, but the fact that the boat was in communication with other steamships may have indicated that she had got off all the messages she wanted to send. He figured the *Titanic*'s position was 1,080 miles from New York when she struck the berg and about 600 miles from Halifax.

Timeline of the Ship's Messages

No word was received from the distressed ship until the middle of the forenoon, which it was given out that the contents of a wireless message from the *Titanic* had been received from Montreal. The message stated that at 8:30 o'clock yesterday morning the vessel was afloat and going slowly under her own power toward Halifax and in the direction the *Virginian* was believed to have taken in response to wireless calls.

The message stated that the women and children had been passed into the lifeboats and small craft on the vessel. The message added that the weather was clear and the sea calm. The pumps were being worked to the utmost, although it was said that the forward hold was filled with water-tight compartments and was standing

Outside the White Star Line offices in New York City, a crowd waits for news about the fate of the passengers on *Titanic*. (© **FPG/Hulton Archive/Getty Images.**)

the strain well, and it was said, if these compartments held out the vessel would reach the shore in safety.

This was the first word that had come to the office, although a message, it was declared, had been received from the *Olympic* saying that she was in wireless communication with the *Titanic*. At 11 o'clock Mr. Franklin told reporters that no more information had been received, but he was sure the bulkhead would hold. A second message, it was announced, was received from Capt. Haddock of the *Olympic*, stating that the *Parisian* and the

> 'Anxiously awaiting information: full particulars; probable disposition of passengers.'

Carpathia had reached the *Titanic*. Mr. Franklin sent this message to Capt. Smith of the *Titanic*:

> Anxiously awaiting information: full particulars; probable disposition of passengers.

The Scene at the White Star Line Office

There was comparatively little excitement then at the White Star offices. The inquirers began to gather early, and there was a crowd waiting when the office doors were opened, shortly before 9 o'clock. After the first of them were reassured and departed to await word from the line, others began to arrive, and all day long there was a continual stream of persons passing in. No one seemed to realize that such a disaster was possible, and, while there was anxiety on the part of all, no real fear was displayed for the ultimate saving of all on board. "The bulkhead must surely hold" was repeated again and again during the day.

Down the steerage department there were many inquiries, and to these the same story of the impossibility of any loss of life was repeated. Among the numerous persons who inquired as to the condition of the damaged boat at the White Star offices was W.H. Force, the father of Mrs. John Jacob Astor. J.G. Dobby, secretary to Mr. Astor, accompanied Mr. Force. Bradley Martin, Jr., was among those who inquired about the boat, but as to whose welfare he was interested in was not learned. Magistrate Robert C. Cornell, whose wife was on the stricken liner, sent one of his court attendants. Ex-Senator Clark was also seen at the office, but officials of the line said he had no relatives on board the *Titanic*, but had come to the office to arrange for transportation.

VIEWPOINT 5

The Remains of *Titanic* Are Finally Discovered Seventy-Three Years Later

Science and Its Times

The *Titanic* shipwreck was located by a team led by Robert D. Ballard in 1985. The following viewpoint describes that event. The authors write that there were a number of challenges, including the lack of precise data about the wreck's location and the depth of the ocean in the search area. However, the search yielded important scientific information about deep-sea research, and the two initial expeditions to *Titanic*'s remains provided close-up photographic evidence for further study. The authors also describe the international nature of the expeditions and the cutting-edge, deep-sea vehicles used. *Science and Its Times* is a seven-volume set, with an interdisciplinary approach

---

SOURCE. "Remains of the RMS *Titanic* Discovered," *Science and Its Times*. Edited by Neil Schlager and Josh Lauer, vol. 7, March 5, 2009.

to teaching science and history, edited by Neil Schlager and Josh Lauer.

In 1985 a joint French and American team found the submerged wreckage of the *Titanic*, the famed luxury liner that struck an iceberg and sank on April 14, 1912. More than 1,500 passengers and crew perished in the wreck. Using a revolutionary sonar vehicle system and a submersible camera-outfitted robot called *Argo* during the expedition, representatives of the U.S. Woods Hole Oceanographic Institution and the French Research Institute for the Exploration of the Sea (IFREMER) located the remains of the *Titanic* on September 1, 1985, after a 56-day search. The *Titanic* rested some 2.5 miles (4 km) beneath the ocean surface and about 350 miles (563 km) from the coast of Nova Scotia in the North Atlantic. Return trips by multiple investigators have yielded ghostly images of rust-encrusted wreckage along with additional data support various hypothesis about the exact sequence of events and extent of damage that caused the vessel to sink. . . . The tragedy and drama of the historical shipwreck caught the attention of Robert D. Ballard, a marine geologist at the Woods Hole Oceanographic Institution and head of its Deep Submergence Laboratory. He spent 13 years searching for the shipwreck before finding the *Titanic* during a joint expedition with IFREMER in 1985. Ballard and Jean-Louis Michel of IFREMER were the chief scientists of the expedition.

> Both the search for the *Titanic* and its findings have important ramifications.

The scientists had a difficult time finding the *Titanic* for several reasons. The exact location of the *Titanic* was unknown. When the *Carpathia* began picking up survivors, the *Titanic* had already sunk and the lifeboats had likely floated a considerable distance from the shipwreck site. In addition, the sea in the area was more than 2 miles (3.2 km) deep, making impossible anything but dives with highly advanced equipment that could survive the great pressures of the depths.

The Challenge of Locating the Wreck

In 1985 the American component of the joint expedition embarked aboard the U.S. Navy research vessel *Knorr* to scan a 150-square-mile (389-square-kilometer) area in the north Atlantic Ocean for the shipwreck. The French team, which had arrived earlier, was aboard another research vessel, the *Le Suroit*. The combined crew used both sonar devices and remote TV cameras to view the ocean floor. Crew members aboard the *Knorr* rotated turns watching the images relayed from the cameras. Fifty-six days into the expedition—at 1 AM on September 1, 1985—the crew member watching the images stopped and said, "Wreckage," followed a second later by shouting, "Bingo!" The crew on watch erupted in cheers.

Both the search for the *Titanic* and its findings have important ramifications. They have demonstrated advancements in undersea exploration, while shining some light on the final moments of the *Titanic*.

Key Findings with *Argo* and SAR

The joint expedition had several key components. One was the *Argo*, a robot search vehicle that contained cameras, sonar devices, timing systems and other electronic equipment. The expedition was actually a testing ground for the *Argo*, which was developed in Ballard's lab. The navy wanted to develop the *Argo* as a tool to find lost submarines and perform deep-sea intelligence missions. On the *Titanic* expedition, however, *Argo*'s primary duty was to locate the shipwreck. The *Argo*, towed by the *Knorr*, skimmed the ocean floor, taking pictures, collecting data, and sending specimens up to the *Knorr*. On the

Titanic Was Found During Secret Cold War Navy Mission

The 1985 discovery of the *Titanic* stemmed from a secret United States Navy investigation of two wrecked nuclear submarines, according to the oceanographer who found the infamous ocean liner. . . . [Oceanographer Robert] Ballard met with the Navy in 1982 to request funding to develop the robotic submersible technology he needed to find the *Titanic*. . . . Ronald Thunman, then the deputy chief of naval operations for submarine warfare, told Ballard the military was interested in the technology—but for the purpose of investigating the wreckage of the U.S.S. *Thresher* and U.S.S. *Scorpion*.

Since Ballard's technology would be able to reach the sunken subs and take pictures, the oceanographer agreed to help out.

He then asked the Navy if he could search for the *Titanic*, which was located between the two wrecks. . . . Once Ballard had completed his mission—if time was left—Thunman said, Ballard could do what he wanted, but never gave him explicit permission to search for the *Titanic*.

SOURCE. *John Roach, "*Titanic *Was Found During Secret Cold War Navy Mission,"* National Geographic News, *June 2, 2008.*

surface, scientists watched and waited. It was the *Argo* that transmitted the first images of the *Titanic*.

The French team relied mostly on SAR, a sonar search vehicle that on every pass scanned a swath of ocean floor a half-mile (0.8-km) wide. As it turned out, the SAR had come within 900 feet (274 m) of the *Titanic* before the

French ship left the expedition in early August, a month before the *Titanic* was discovered.

Following the discovery of the ocean liner's resting place, the joint U.S.-French team launched a remote camera capable of taking high-resolution still photographs. Those photographs provided detailed images of the so-called debris field, which held the remains of the *Titanic*. The photographs showed torn and twisted pieces of the ship alongside scattered anchor chains, plates, and possibly intact bottles of wine.

Return to the Wreck with *Alvin* and *Jason Jr.*

Nearly a year after the discovery of the *Titanic*, Ballard returned to the shipwreck site. This time he brought *Alvin*, a manned deep-sea submersible. *Alvin* includes a titanium crew compartment that is 7 feet (2.1 m) in diameter, and can hold up to three people and a variety of equipment. Ballard also brought the much smaller *Jason Jr.*, a robot submarine developed in his lab for the navy. Unlike the *Argo*, *Alvin* and *Jason Jr.* are not physically connected to the mother ship at the surface. *Jason Jr.* is an unmanned vehicle controlled by a scientist aboard *Alvin*. *Jason Jr.* can travel up to 200 feet (61 m) from the *Alvin* during operation. While scientists could get close to the *Titanic* in *Alvin*, the shipwreck's wires, railings, and other obstacles made those types of ventures dangerous. *Jason Jr.*, however, was small enough to negotiate around the obstacles and even enter the ship, and its single camera could relay pictures directly to the scientist controlling it.

During the *Alvin* and *Jason Jr.* missions, both experienced problems and taught the scientists more about deep-sea research. *Alvin* took its first trip to the *Titanic* without *Jason Jr.* After a 2.5-hour free fall through the water to the ocean floor—the free-fall descent saves energy for sea-bottom travel—*Alvin*'s batteries developed leaks and its sonar failed. The *Alvin*'s crew brought the submersible back to the surface for a night of repairs. The following day, *Alvin* worked and the deep-sea mission went smoothly until the final ascent to the ship. Attached to *Alvin* during the ascent, *Jason Jr.* came loose at the ocean surface, and divers had to jump in and save the little robot, which was no longer under *Alvin*'s control. Again, the scientists and technicians had to make quick repairs. Subsequent dives with *Alvin* and *Jason Jr.* were successful and provided close-up and "aerial" views of the wreckage.

Many of the photographs from these expeditions to the *Titanic* provided clues to the ship's demise.

Many of the photographs from these expeditions to the *Titanic* provided clues to the ship's demise. For instance, photographs indicate that one of the ship's four giant stacks was ripped from its foundation and fell across the bridge as the ship sank. The collapsing stack also pulled the mast backward. Survivors reported seeing multimillionaire businessman John Jacob Astor for the last time standing approximately where the stack fell. Astor, who had purchased passage on the *Titanic* for himself and his new wife as part of their honeymoon, likely died there on the deck.

Other photographs of the shipwreck show that the entire debris field astern of the *Titanic* is filled with remnants of one area of the hull. From these photographs and other evidence, the research team concluded that the hull had been torn asunder. The photographs and data clearly show two major sections of the *Titanic* some 1,800 feet (549 m) apart, which supports survivor accounts that the ship split in half as it sank.

After analyzing the research team's evidence, Dr. Ballard concluded that these initial violent events at the surface were followed by a slow fall to the depths of the ocean, where the *Titanic* settled without much fur-

ther damage. Other authorities had previously hypothesized that the *Titanic* underwent a 100-mile-per-hour (161 kph) collision with the sea floor.

Argo, a deep-sea craft developed by oceanographer Robert Ballard and his team, descends toward the *Titanic* wreck in 1985. (© **Emory Kristof/ National Geographic/ Getty Images.**)

A Boon for Deep-Sea Research

In addition to providing insight into events on the night the *Titanic* sank, the expedition demonstrated that an unmanned submarine, and *Jason Jr.* in particular, could be a boon for deep-sea oceanographic research. Ballard argued that if control of these submarines could be extended well beyond the 200-foot (61-m) limit for *Jason Jr.*, eventually technicians would be able to remain aboard the research vessel and control the robot vehicles from there. Dangerous manned missions to the ocean depths, then, would become obsolete. In 1995 Ballard was part of the team that discovered the underwater wreckage of the aircraft carrier U.S.S. *Yorktown.* For that expedition, the team used a remotely operated submersible called the advanced tethered vehicle to reach the wreckage on the floor of the north-central Pacific, some 16,650 feet (5,075 m) down.

The search for the *Titanic* was . . . . an attempt to disguise the clandestine inspection of two sunken Cold War era nuclear submarines.

In 2003, a Ballard-led expedition found the wreck of U.S. Naval vessel, *PT-109* off the Solomon Islands. *PT-109*, a small motor torpedo boat commanded during World War II by then-Lieutenant (Junior Grade) John F. Kennedy—later to be elected President of the United States in 1960—was rammed and sunk during combat in August 1943.

In 2008, Ballard confirmed long-standing rumors that the search for the *Titanic* was, in part, both genuine exploration, and an attempt to disguise the clandestine inspection of two sunken Cold War era nuclear submarines, USS *Thresher* and USS *Scorpion,* for the United States Navy.

VIEWPOINT 6

An Exhibitions Company Gains Legal Ownership of the *Titanic* Wreck

Globe Newswire

The following viewpoint reports on a 2011 court ruling that granted ownership of *Titanic* artifacts to RMS Titanic Inc. (RMST), a company that creates traveling exhibitions. The viewpoint explains that the ruling applies to artifacts recovered from the wreck after 1987 and that the US government secured certain concessions to ensure that the artifacts will be conserved in a manner consistent with historic and preservation standards. According to the viewpoint, RMST already had title to artifacts salvaged before 1987, and the combined value of its *Titanic* holdings is more than $189 million. The company intends to capitalize on the court ruling in time for the 2012 centennial anniversary of the sinking of *Titanic*, according to an

---

SOURCE. "Premier Exhibitions, Inc. Receives Title to *Titanic* Artifacts," Globe Newswire, August 17, 2011.

RMST executive quoted. Globe Newswire is one of the world's largest newswire distribution networks, specializing in corporate press releases, financial disclosures, and multimedia content for investors and the general public.

Atlanta, Aug. 17, 2011—Premier Exhibitions, Inc. (the "Company"), a leading presenter of museum-quality touring exhibitions around the world, announced on Monday, August 15 that the United States District Court for the Eastern District of Virginia, Norfolk Division, (the "Court") has granted title to RMS Titanic, Inc. ("RMST"), a wholly owned subsidiary of the Company, for approximately 3,000 artifacts recovered from the wreck of *Titanic* during RMST's expeditions conducted in 1993, 1994, 1996, 1998, 2000, and 2004 (the "Post 1987 Artifacts"). Title to the Post 1987 Artifacts was granted through the issuance of an "in-specie" salvage award in an opinion issued by the Court on August 15.

In August of 2010, the Court awarded the Company, through RMST, 100% of the approximately $110 million fair market value of the Post 1987 Artifacts, based on an updated appraisal of the artifacts conducted in 2009. At the time, the Court had reserved the right to determine the manner in which to pay the award, either through a cash award of the fair market value (to be raised via judicial sale) or an in-specie award granting title to the Post 1987 Artifacts to RMST subject to certain covenants and conditions agreed to by the Company.

> 'Conditions ensure that this collection of artifacts . . . will be conserved and . . . curated consistent with . . . historic preservation standards.'

Premier Exhibitions, Inc., through RMST, has been the Salvor-in-Possession of the *Titanic* wreck site since 1994, giving it the sole and exclusive rights to recover artifacts from the wreck. In 1993, a French maritime tribunal awarded RMST title to the approximately 1,800 artifacts recovered in 1987 (the "1987 Artifacts"). In 2007, these artifacts were appraised at over $35 million. The covenants and conditions implemented by yesterday's court ruling were not applicable at the time of the 2007 appraisal.

Government Conditions for *Titanic* Artifacts

Title to the Post 1987 Artifacts comes with certain covenants and conditions drafted and negotiated by the Company and the United States government. These covenants and conditions govern the maintenance and future disposition of the artifacts. James Delgado, Director of Maritime Heritage with NOAA's Office of National Marine Sanctuaries, stated "The covenants and conditions were initially proposed by RMST, negotiated with NOAA and the Department of Commerce of the United States through the United States Attorney, and then finalized with RMST and the Court. The public interest in *Titanic* has been recognized by the Court and RMST and these covenants and conditions ensure that this collection of artifacts recovered from *Titanic* will be conserved and curated consistent with current international and U.S. historic preservation standards." These covenants and conditions include the following:

- The approximately 1,800 "1987 Artifacts" and the approximately 3,000 "Post 1987 Artifacts" must be maintained as a single collection;
- The combined collections can only be sold together, in their entirety, and any buyer would be subject to the same conditions applicable to RMST; and
- RMST must comply with provisions that guarantee the long-term protection of all of the artifacts.

The covenants and conditions could have an impact on the appraised value of the artifacts and on the alternatives the Company has with respect to the assets. However, the Company agreed to and fully understands the covenants and conditions, and is evaluating all alternatives to utilize the assets to maximize their value to shareholders.

Appraised Value of the Artifacts

Based upon the aforementioned appraisals, the total value to Premier Exhibitions, Inc. of the "1987 Artifacts" and the "Post 1987 Artifacts" approximates $145 million, not including the intangible assets associated with the collection. The actual value of the artifacts may differ materially today given the current market for historic collectibles and the covenants and conditions imposed by the Court. These assets have never been held for public sale and their true fair market value would be based in large part on the overall market for historic collectibles. The *Titanic* artifacts represent a one-of-a-kind collection.

> The [artifacts] and intellectual property have an appraised value of approximately $189 million.

In addition to holding title to the 1987 Artifacts and Post 1987 Artifacts collections, RMST also owns significant work product and other intellectual property related to *Titanic*, such as film footage of the wreck site, digital archives, dive records, mapping of the wreck site, a valuable database and other unique elements obtained over the last 23 years by RMST and the Company. The 2007 appraisal found approximately $44 million in additive value to the collection attributable to this intellectual property and to the Company's and RMST's undertakings, such as the costs of salvage, lab operations and exhibition. This appraised valuation does not include any of the new work product and intellectual property obtained in the Company's 2010 expedition to the wreck site.

Together, the 1987 Artifacts, the Post 1987 Artifacts, and the work product and intellectual property have an appraised value of approximately $189 million. This estimated value of the collection pre-dates the intellectual property acquired from the 2010 expedition and any additional artifacts or intellectual property that may be obtained in the future.

The Company's Future Plans

The Company wants to thank all of the individuals who have assisted us in achieving this outcome with special recognition to David J. Bederman, the K.H. Gyr Professor of Private International Law at Emory University School of Law. Professor Bederman became our chief maritime law expert in 2004 and was instrumental in shaping the legal strategy that has resulted in a positive outcome in this case.

Christopher Davino, Premier Exhibitions, Inc.'s President and Chief Executive, stated, "We are delighted that the Court has rendered its long-awaited decision on this critical matter, and that the Company now possesses title to the approximately 5,000 artifacts that have been recovered and conserved from *Titanic* since 1987. We remain committed to the long-term protection and preservation of these historical artifacts and *Titanic*'s wreck site, and we look forward to continuing our role as Salvor-in-Possession of *Titanic* as we have since 1994. This ruling is especially timely in view of the upcoming 100th Anniversary of the *Titanic* sinking in 2012, and our intention is to fully capitalize on the opportunities that this milestone anniversary affords our *Titanic* brand."

RMS Titanic, Inc., a wholly owned subsidiary of Premier Exhibitions, Inc., is the only company permitted by law to recover objects from the wreck of *Titanic*. The Company was granted Salvor-In-Possession rights to the wreck of *Titanic* by the Court in 1994 and has conducted seven research and recovery expeditions to *Titanic* recovering more than 5,500 artifacts. In the summer of 2010, RMS Titanic, Inc. conducted a ground-breaking expedition to *Titanic* 25 years after its discovery, to undertake innovative 3D video recording, data gathering and other technical measures so as to virtually raise *Titanic*, preserving the legacy of the Ship for all time.

CHAPTER 2

Controversies Surrounding the *Titanic* Disaster

VIEWPOINT 1

Negligence Caused the *Titanic* Disaster

US Senate Committee on Commerce

Hearings conducted by a special subcommittee of the United States Senate began in New York City on April 19, 1912—the day after *Titanic* survivors arrived—and concluded a month later in Washington, DC. The following viewpoint summarizes the Senate's key findings after hearing testimony from eighty-two witnesses, including: the insufficient training of staff and testing of *Titanic* before its maiden voyage, ignored ice warnings, misuse of the scarce lifeboats, the ship's high speed at the time of the accident, and the failure of the watertight bulkhead compartments. The Senate concludes that new laws are needed to ensure passenger safety and details a number of recommendations. Some of its recommendations, such as those related to lifeboat capacity and ship telecommunications, are still reflected in present-day regulations.

Photo on previous page: The prow of the *Titanic*, lying about 12,500 feet below the surface of the Atlantic Ocean, is seen on an image captured during a deep-sea dive to the wreck site in 1995. (© **Ralph White/ Corbis.**)

SOURCE. "*Titanic* Disaster: Report of the Committee on Commerce," United States Senate, Report No. 806. Washington, DC: Government Printing Office, 1912.

We find that the *Titanic* was a White Star steamer and was owned by the Oceanic Steam Navigation Co., of England, all of the stock of which company is in turn owned by the International Navigation Co. (Ltd.), of England, and the stock of that company, in turn, is owned by the International Mercantile Marine Co., an American corporation, organized under the laws of New Jersey. . . .

The *Titanic* was built by Harland and Wolff, of Belfast, Ireland. No restriction as to limit of cost was placed upon the builders. She was launched May 31, 1911. She was a vessel of 46,328 tons register; her length was 882.6 feet, and her breadth was 92.6 feet. Her boat deck and bridge were 70 feet above the waterline. She was, according to the testimony of President [J. Bruce] Ismay, "especially constructed to float with her two largest watertight compartments full of water."

The vessel, fully equipped, cost £1,500,000 sterling, or about $7,500,000 [about $36 million in 2014 dollars].

At the time of the accident the vessel carried insurance of £1,000,000 sterling or about $5,000,000, the remaining risk being carried by the company's insurance fund.

The *Titanic* was a duplicate of the *Olympic*, which is owned by the same company, with a single exception of her passenger accommodations, and was built to accommodate 2,599 passengers, with additional accommodations for officers and crew numbering 903 persons.

> Many of the crew did not join the ship until a few hours before sailing.

Insufficient Testing and Training

The committee finds from the evidence that between six and seven hours was spent in making trial tests of this vessel at Belfast Lough on Monday, the 1st of April last [1911]. A few turning circles were made, compasses adjusted, and she steamed a short time under approximately a full head of steam, but the ship was not driven at her full speed. . . . Many of the crew did not join the ship until a few hours before sailing, and the only drill while the vessel lay at Southampton or on the voyage consisted in lowering two lifeboats on the starboard side into the water, which boats were again hoisted to the boat deck within a half hour. No boat list designating the stations of members of the crew was posted until several days after sailing from Southampton, boatmen being left in ignorance of their proper stations until the following Friday morning.

On Wednesday morning, the day the ship sailed from Southampton, Capt. Clark, a representative of the British Board of Trade, came aboard and, after spending a brief time, issued the necessary certificate to permit sailing.

The US Senate Investigating Committee questions Harold Thomas Cottam, a *Carpathia* wireless operator, during the 1912 *Titanic* disaster hearings in New York City. (© **Universal History Archive/Getty Images.**)

An Insufficient Number of Lifeboats

The *Titanic* was fitted with 16 sets of double-acting boat davits of modern type, capable of handling 2 or 3 boats per set of davits. The davits were thus capable of handling 48 boats, whereas the ship carried but 16 lifeboats and 4 collapsibles, fulfilling all the requirements of the British Board of Trade. The *Titanic* was provided with 14 lifeboats, of capacity for 65 persons each, or 910 persons; 2 emergency sea boats, of capacity for 35 persons each, or 70 persons; 4 collapsible boats, of capacity for 49 persons each, or 196 persons. Total lifeboat capacity, 1,176. There was ample lifebelt equipment for all. . . .

Ignored Ice Warnings

During the entire voyage the weather was clear, with the single exception of 10 minutes of fog, and the sea was calm throughout the voyage, with sunshine the whole of each day and bright starlight every night. No untoward incident marred the trip. Greetings were frequently exchanged with passing vessels by appropriate signals.

On the third day out ice warnings were received by the wireless operators on the *Titanic*, and the testimony is conclusive that at least three of these warnings came direct to the commander of the *Titanic* on the day of the accident, the first about noon, from the *Baltic*, of the White Star Line. It will be noted that this message places icebergs within five miles of the track which the *Titanic* was following, and near the place where the accident occurred. . . . The ice positions so definitely reported to the *Titanic* just preceding the accident located ice on both sides of the track or lane which the *Titanic* was following, and in her immediate vicinity. No general discussion took place among the officers; no conference was called to consider these warnings; no heed was given

“Ice [was reported] on both sides of the track or lane which the *Titanic* was following, and in her immediate vicinity.”

to them. The speed was not relaxed, the lookout was not increased, and the only vigilance displayed by the officer of the watch was by instructions to the lookouts to keep "a sharp lookout for ice." It should be said, however, that the testimony shows that Capt. [Edward] Smith remarked to Officer [Charles] Lightoller, who was the officer doing duty on the bridge until 10 o'clock ship's time, or 8.27 o'clock New York time, "If it was in a slight degree hazy there would be no doubt we should have to go very slowly," and "If in the slightest degree doubtful, let me know." The evidence is that it was exceptionally clear. There was no haze, and the ship's speed was not reduced. . . .

Iceberg Collision and Damage

At 11.46 PM ship's time, or 10.13 PM New York time, Sunday evening, April 14, the lookout signaled the bridge and telephoned the Officer of the watch, "Iceberg right ahead." The Officer of the watch, Mr. [William McMaster] Murdoch, immediately ordered the Quartermaster at the wheel to put the helm "hard astarboard," and reversed the engines; but while the Sixth Officer standing behind the Quartermaster at the wheel reported to Officer Murdoch "The helm is hard astarboard," the *Titanic* struck the ice. The impact, while not violent enough to disturb the passengers or crew, or to arrest the ship's progress, rolled the vessel slightly and tore the steel plating above the turn of the bilge.

The testimony shows that coincident with the collision air was heard whistling or hissing from the overflow pipe to the forepeak tank, indicating the escape of air from that tank because of the inrush of water. Practically at once, the forepeak tank, No. 1 hold, No. 2 hold, No. 3 hold, and forward boiler room, filled with water, the presence of which was immediately reported from the mail room and the racquet court and trunk room in No. 3 hold, and also from the firemen's quarters in No. 1

hold. Leading Fireman Barrett saw the water rushing into the forward fireroom from a tear about two feet above the stokehold floor plates and about twenty feet below the waterline, which tear extended two feet into the coal bunker at the forward end of the second fireroom.

The reports received by the Captain after various inspections of the ship must have acquainted him promptly with its serious condition, and when interrogated by President Ismay, he so expressed himself. It is believed, also, that this serious condition was promptly realized by the chief engineer and by the builders' representative, Mr. Andrews, none of whom survived.

Bulkhead Compartments Not Watertight

Under this added weight of water the bow of the ship sank deeper and deeper into the water, and through the open hatch leading from the mail room, and through other openings, water promptly overflowed E deck, below which deck the third, fourth, fifth, sixth, seventh, and eighth transverse bulkheads ended, and thus flooded the compartments abaft No. 3 hold.

> The supposedly watertight compartments were NOT watertight, and the sinking of the vessel followed.

The *Titanic* was fitted with 15 transverse watertight bulkheads, only 1, the first bulkhead from forward, extended to the uppermost continuous deck, C; bulkheads Nos. 2, 10, 11, 12, 13, 14, and 15 extended to the second continuous deck, D; and bulkheads Nos. 3, 4, 5, 6, 7, 8, and 9 extended only to the third continuous deck, E. The openings through deck E were not designed for watertight closing, as the evidence shows that flooding over deck E contributed largely to the sinking of the vessel. The bulkheads above described divided the ship into 16 main watertight compartments, and the ship was so arranged that any 2 main compartments might be flooded without in any way involving the safety of the ship. As before stated, the testimony shows that the 5 extreme forward compartments were flooded practically immediately, and under such circumstances, by reason of the non watertight character of the deck at which the transverse bulkheads ended, the supposedly watertight compartments were NOT watertight, and the sinking of the vessel followed. . . .

Misuse of Lifeboats

When Captain Smith received the reports as to the water entering the ship, he promptly gave the order to clear away the lifeboats, and later orders were given to put women and children into the boats. During this time distress rockets were fired at frequent intervals.

The lack of preparation was at this time most noticeable. There was no system adopted for loading the boats; there was great indecision as to the deck from which boats were to be loaded; there was wide diversity of opinion as to the number of the crew necessary to man each boat; there was no direction whatever as to the number of passengers to be carried by each boat, and no uniformity in loading them. On one side only women and children were put in the boats, while on the other side there was almost an equal proportion of men and women put into the boats, the women and children being given the preference in all cases. The failure to utilize all lifeboats to their recognized capacity for safety unquestionably resulted in the needless sacrifice of several hundred lives which might otherwise have been saved.

The vessel was provided with lifeboats, as above stated, for 1,176 persons, while but 706 were saved. Only a few of the ship's lifeboats were fully loaded, while others were but partially filled. Some were loaded at the boat deck, and some at the A deck, and these were successfully lowered to the water. The twentieth boat was washed overboard when the forward part of the ship was submerged, and in its overturned condition served as a

THE *TITANIC'S* LIFEBOATS

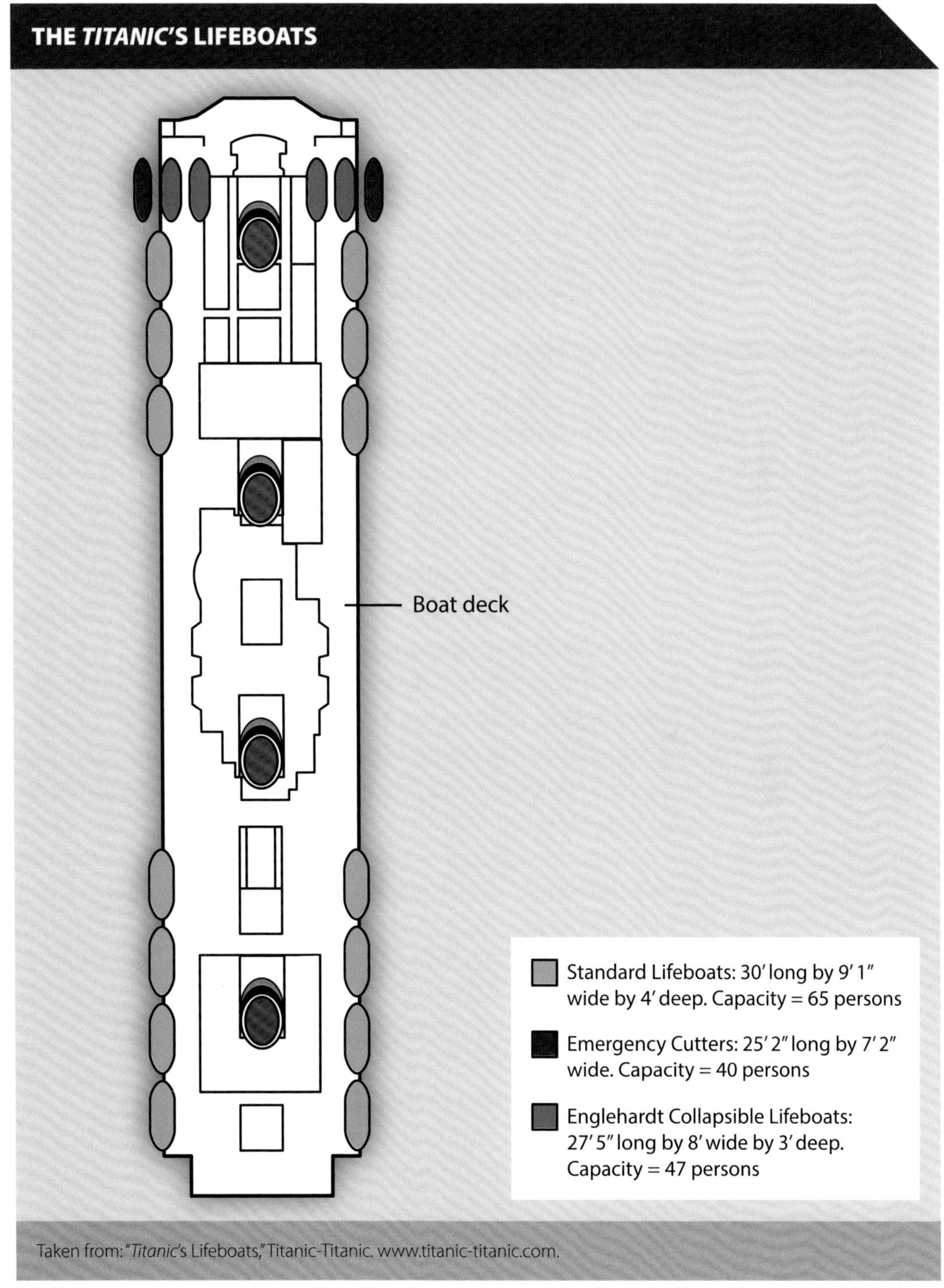

Taken from: "*Titanic*'s Lifeboats," Titanic-Titanic. www.titanic-titanic.com.

life raft for about 30 people, including Second Officer Lightoller, Wireless Operators [Harold] Bride and [Jack] Phillips (the latter dying before rescue), passengers Col. Gracie and Mr. Jack Thayer, and others of the crew, who climbed upon it from the water at about the time the ship disappeared. . . . In the reports of the survivors there are marked differences of opinion as to the number carried by each lifeboat. In No. 1, for instance, one survivor reports ten in all. The seaman in charge reports 7 crew and 14 to 20 passengers. The officer who loaded this boat estimated that from 3 to 5 women and 22 men were aboard. Accepting the minimum report as made by any one survivor in every boat, the total far exceeds the actual number picked up by the *Carpathia*.

> Under proper discipline . . . it would have been possible to have saved many [more] lives.

The testimony is definite that, except in isolated instances, there was no panic. In loading boats no distinction was made between first, second, and third class passengers, although the proportion of lost is larger among third class passengers than in either of the other classes. Women and children, without discrimination, were given preference.

Your committee believes that under proper discipline the survivors could have been concentrated into fewer boats after reaching the water, and we think that it would have been possible to have saved many lives had those in charge of the boats thus released returned promptly to the scene of the disaster. . . .

Final Recommendations

The committee finds that this accident clearly indicates the necessity of additional legislation to secure safety of life at sea.

By statute the United States accepts reciprocally the inspection certificates of foreign countries having inspection laws approximating those of the United States. Unless there is early revision of inspection laws of foreign countries along the lines laid down hereinafter, the committee deems it proper that such reciprocal arrangements be terminated, and that no vessel shall be licensed to carry passengers from ports of the United States until all regulations and requirements of the laws of the United States have been fully complied with.

The committee recommends that [laws] be so amended as to definitely require sufficient lifeboats to accommodate every passenger and every member of the crew. . . . The committee recommends the assignment of passengers and crew to lifeboats before sailing. . . . The committee recommends that every ocean steamship carrying 100 or more passengers be required to carry 2 electric searchlights.

The committee finds that this catastrophe makes glaringly apparent the necessity for regulation of radiotelegraphy. There must be an operator on duty at all times, day and night, to insure the immediate receipt of all distress, warning, or other important calls. Direct communication either by clear-speaking telephone, voice tube, or messenger must be provided between the wireless room and the bridge, so that the operator does not have to leave his station. There must be definite legislation to prevent interference by amateurs, and to secure secrecy of radiograms or wireless messages. There must be some source of auxiliary power, either storage battery or oil engine, to insure the operation of the wireless installation until the wireless room is submerged. . . . All steel ocean and coastwise seagoing ships carrying 100 or more passengers should have a watertight skin inboard of the outside plating, extending not less than 10 percent of the load draft above the full-load waterline. . . . All steel ocean and coastwise seagoing ships carrying 100 or more passengers should have bulkheads so spaced that any two adjacent compartments of the ship may be flooded without destroying the floatability or stability of the ship. . . . All watertight bulkheads and decks should be proportioned to withstand, without material permanent deflection, a water pressure equal to 5 feet more than the full height of the bulkhead. Bulkheads of novel dimensions or scantlings should be tested by being subjected to actual water pressure.

VIEWPOINT 2

The *Titanic* Investigation Raised Issues of International Law and Jurisdiction

House of Lords, UK Parliament

In the following viewpoint, the British Parliament discusses the ongoing US Senate investigation into the *Titanic* disaster in 1912. Members of Parliament (MPs) raise a number of critical questions, including whether international law or custom allow another country to investigate a British vessel lost at sea and the potential effect of the US hearings on a subsequent British inquiry. Some MPs concede that *Titanic* was not entirely British; although it sailed under the British flag, it was owned by an American company. Other MPs note that the United States enjoys a close relationship with Great Britain and that it is necessary and reasonable for a country to investigate an incident in which its citizens have perished. The discussion concludes with an acknowledgment that the issue of national ownership of a

---

SOURCE. House of Lords, UK Parliament, "The Wreck of the *Titanic*," *Hansard: The House of Lords Debates*, vol. 11, no. cc 8518, April 25, 1912.

ship is not a mere technicality and that changes may be needed to international law to clarify legal jurisdiction.

Earl Stanhope: My Lords, I rise to ask His Majesty's Government—

1. Whether it is in accordance with the customs of International Law and the usual practice that an inquiry should be held in a foreign country into the loss of a vessel sailing under the British flag which is shipwrecked on the high seas.
2. Whether the United States Government communicated with His Majesty's Government before instituting the inquiry into the disaster to the *Titanic*; and whether the Governments of any other Powers who had citizens amongst the passengers have notified their intention of holding an inquiry into the matter.
3. Whether the evidence given before the Committee in the United States will be admissible as evidence at the inquiry to be held in this country.

I see by this morning's [April 25, 1912] papers that it was stated yesterday in another place in reply to a Question concerning the inquiry now being held at Washington [DC], that this was the first occasion on which a foreign Government had held an inquiry into the loss of a ship sailing under the British flag. I think the House will desire to know whether the situation is in accord with the customs of international law, and, further whether His Majesty's Government were approached with regard to the inquiry now proceeding in America before it was actually instituted. A departure of such magnitude from the practice to which we have been accustomed is of vital importance, not only to British shipping companies, but still more to the officers and men on ships sailing under the British flag. If this inquiry is taken as a precedent it is very difficult to say where we shall end. If the United States Government have already approached the responsible Department in this country it is obvious that the question of precedent must already have been raised, and in that case no doubt the House will be able to get some information on the matter.

The American Justification for the Inquiry

So far as I have been able to see, this inquiry at Washington had, perhaps, two grounds of justification. The first is that, the shipping company which owned the *Titanic* was not altogether a British company. I believe it is partly American in its management, and therefore an inquiry could be held by the country which was largely interested in the shipping concern. Obviously, if that decision is accepted it raises an extraordinary situation, because it strikes at the root of the whole question of the position of the Mercantile Marine in time of war. It is obvious that a shipping company which is under such dual management would, in time of war, promptly hoist the flag of the neutral Power if one of these Powers happened to be neutral and the other belligerent. That would raise the question, which would be difficult to deal with, as to whether the ship belonged to the neutral Power or the belligerent Power.

> The only other justification which might be advanced . . . is the terrible loss of life among American citizens.

The only other justification which might be advanced for the inquiry in America is the terrible loss of life among American citizens. But if that is to hold good as a reason for this inquiry, it is obvious that every other nation which had citizens on board the *Titanic*, who unfortunately are no more, would be justified in holding an inquiry of a similar character. To put it shortly, I can imagine nothing more deplorable for the survivors of a great disaster than to be dragged about from one country to another attending inquiries and giving evidence of an experience so awful.

There is another point, and perhaps the most important point of all, and that is . . . whether the evidence given before the Committee in the United States will be admissible as evidence at the inquiry to be held in this country. The feelings of the officers and men who have given evidence at the American inquiry are naturally worthy of great consideration; but far more important still is the result with regard to the evidence to be given at the official inquiry in this country. I believe that noble and learned Lords will agree that evidence given at a first inquiry is of far more value and is far more to be depended upon than evidence given at a later inquiry. There are obvious reasons for such a view. If the evidence given before the inquiry now being held in America is to be admissible at the official inquiry in this country, no doubt His Majesty's Government have made arrangements for an official transcript of that evidence to be made for the purpose of the inquiry to be held here. If the evidence is not to be held admissible, then the inquiry here will obviously be penalised by not being the first inquiry held into this great disaster.

'I do not wish to go into the question of whether the American inquiry was right or wrong.'

I do not wish to go into the question of whether the American inquiry was right or wrong. Fortunately, the relations between this country and the United States are so friendly that no international question can possibly arise. Our relations with the United States Government are friendly; our relations with the people of the United States are, perhaps, even more so. But undoubtedly there is a certain amount of feeling in this country in regard to the inquiry which is now being held. I do not think that feeling is strong. It has certainly not been as forcibly worded as if the situation had been reversed. Imagine that it had been an American ship which had been lost and that we were holding an inquiry here and detaining American citizens from going back to their own inquiry and possibly asking for documents from United States shipping companies to be laid before our inquiry. In that case I think things would be said in the United States which everyone in this country would be likely to regret.

Moreover if the action of the United States is to be taken as a precedent by other Powers, we may get to a serious situation indeed. If our relations with another Power were strained, and if, alas, there were a similar accident, I think we should hold very strong views indeed if we found that our citizens were being detained in that country for an inquiry into the loss of a British ship purely and simply because a number of citizens of that other Power had been aboard. Though such a disaster as this draws the whole world together, still these matters, unless threshed out before the situation arises, do give points for friction. I have therefore put these Questions on the Paper not only to elucidate the present position, but also, if possible, to make clear what is to be our position in the future.

The Necessity for a US Inquiry

Viscount Morley: My Lords, . . . the noble Earl asks, "Is there a right for another country to inquire into the circumstances of the wreck of a British ship on the high seas?" There is no doubt that any State may institute an inquiry about the wreck of a foreign vessel in which the lives of its own citizens have been lost, without any departure from international law, though we are not aware that any such case has arisen before. The answer to the second Question is simple. Communications have not been addressed to the Government of the United States, and no intimations or communications have been received from any other Powers by us.

On the point of the admissibility of evidence, the Wreck Commissioner, Lord Mersey, in this country will be able to receive any information that he thinks will be useful, and will attach to it whatever weight he thinks it deserves, quite independently of what may have happened anywhere else. No doubt he will get all the most direct evidence that he can obtain in the regular course. But the inquiry that Lord Mersey undertakes is different from a trial between parties, and the rules of evidence applicable to litigation are not necessarily adhered to in an inquiry of this kind. As to the detention of witnesses, compelling witnesses to attend, and, maybe, detaining them, powers of that kind, as I am advised, exist in most countries. It is obvious that such powers, existing as they do, should be exercised with full consideration for the witnesses themselves, and also for the necessities of any inquiry at home. We cannot and do not, and I am sure the noble Earl does not, suppose that the Committee of the Senate will overlook the necessity for regard for these fair and reasonable considerations.

> The rules of evidence applicable to litigation are not necessarily adhered to in an inquiry of this kind.

The Marquess of Lansdowne: My Lords, I was glad to hear the noble Viscount admit that my noble friend was justified in putting these Questions on the Paper. They relate to matters which are engaging a great amount of public attention at this moment, and they are matters with regard to which much anxiety is felt in many quarters. I feel sure that my noble friend will not disregard the appeal made to him by the noble Viscount and that he will not press more than is necessary his demand for fuller information. It seems, of course, to most people unusual and not in accordance with precedent that a ship sailing under the British flag and wrecked in midocean should be made the subject of an inquiry of this kind by a foreign Power; but, on the other hand, we have to remember that the circumstances of this case are. I think I am justified in saying, wholly unparalleled both as regards the magnitude of the tragedy and the moving incidents by which it was accompanied. In these circumstances it is, perhaps, not a matter for surprise that public opinion in the United States should have been deeply stirred, and should have insisted upon some such inquiry as that which is now in progress. . . . It was stated in the House of Commons last night by the representative of His Majesty's Government that they were considering whether any diplomatic representations should be made, and it does seem to me that such communications may become necessary to this extent, at all events, that possibly British subjects who have to appear before the Senate Committee may need a certain amount of advice and assistance.

I will go a little further and say that I trust it may be so arranged that the proceedings on the other side of the Atlantic will not be of a kind which will interfere with the proceedings which will have to take place on this side of the Atlantic under circumstances which to most of us suggest that the proceedings here will be more regular in form and more satisfactory in substance than those which are going on at Washington.

But, my Lords, although difficulties may arise in connection with this question, I feel, as I think my noble friend feels, that public opinion on both sides of the Atlantic is sound upon this question, and that on neither side will that public opinion allow two countries connected, as we and the United States are, by the closest ties and also, in this case, by a common sorrow, to fail in their obligations either to the living or to the dead owing to any mere technicalities of international procedure or etiquette.

Ownership "Technicalities"

Lord St. Davids: My Lords, . . . I concur with the sentiment expressed by the noble Marquess that no attempt to get at the facts of this wholly deplorable matter should be hampered by technicalities, but I think it is vital to remember that the *Titanic* was only technically a British ship. She sailed, it is true, under the British flag, but to the best of my belief the company that owned her is entirely and absolutely controlled by an American corporation. The American Shipping Trust undoubtedly owns and controls this Line and can do exactly what it likes with it, although technically it is a British company and flies the British flag. It seems to me that although the *Titanic* flew the British flag, that is a technicality which ought not unduly to weigh with us when we know that it was owned by a foreign company. I cannot help hoping that as the result of the inquiry which is to be held in this country there may be an agreement between the nations of the world that the state of things under which a ship is technically owned in one country and controlled in another should no longer exist, but that the flag and ownership should go together.

"The national character of a ship is by no means a technicality. It is a matter of supreme importance."

The Earl of Halsbury: My Lords, . . . The national character of a ship is by no means a technicality. It is a matter of supreme importance, and a supposed jurisdiction of all the world would be absolutely intolerable. I do not want to enter into a discussion of the matter after what the noble Viscount has said. I feel it cannot do any good, and it might do some mischief.

VIEWPOINT 3

Titanic's Discovery Resulted in a Tangle of Lawsuits

Ricardo Elia

The legal history of *Titanic* from the wreck's discovery in 1985 through 2000 has been a contentious one. In this viewpoint, an archaelogy professor reports that two years after the discovery, artifacts were already being removed, stirring controversy and outrage from at least one *Titanic* survivor. After a number of legal challenges, RMS Titanic Inc. (RMST) gained legal control of the site, and a large number of artifacts and footage from dives to the site were used in TV and film projects. Subsequent legal challenges include lawsuits aimed at prohibiting RMST from excluding others from visiting or capturing images of *Titanic* and preventing the National Oceanic and Atmospheric Administration from creating an international preservation agreement for the site. The author writes that, unfortunately, RMST is primarily interested in mounting profitable exhibitions and maintaining its "in possession" status while sacrificing the

SOURCE. Ricardo Elia, "*Titanic* in the Courts," *Archaeology*, vol. 54, no. 1, January–February, 2011.

archaeological needs of the site. Ricardo Elia is a professor of archaeology at Boston University and a former editor in chief of the *Journal of Field Archaeology*.

On April 15 [1912], the White Star ocean liner RMS *Titanic* sinks on her maiden voyage after striking an iceberg in international waters 400 miles off the coast of Newfoundland. More than 1,500 passengers and crew perish. Claimants in the United Kingdom and United States seek compensation for personal injury, loss of life, and loss of property.

1916. *Titanic*'s owner, Oceanic Steam Navigation Company, pays a total of $664,000 to settle all legal claims.

1985. *Titanic* is discovered on September 1 by a joint expedition of the Woods Hole Oceanographic Institution and the Institute of France for the Research and Exploration of the Sea (IFREMER). American co-leader Robert Ballard makes several dives to the wreck site in the submersible *Alvin*. The team decides not to salvage artifacts from it.

1986. In July, during a second season of exploring the site, Ballard places a plaque on *Titanic*, urging that the site be left undisturbed as a memorial. Congress passes the RMS *Titanic* Maritime Memorial Act, which directs the United States to enter into negotiations with other interested nations to establish guidelines to protect the "scientific, cultural, and historical significance of RMS *Titanic*." The act also expresses the sense of Congress that, pending such an agreement, "no person should physically alter, disturb, or salvage the RMS *Titanic*." The Department of State contacts the United Kingdom, France, and Canada but finds little interest in an agreement.

Removal of Artifacts

1987. IFREMER contracts with Titanic Ventures, a limited partnership, to salvage artifacts from the site. Titanic Ventures makes 32 dives to the site and recovers some 1,800 artifacts. The operation draws protests; *Titanic* survivor Eva Hart decries the "insensitivity and greed" and labels the salvors "fortune hunters, vultures, pirates." Titanic Ventures sells its salvage interests and artifacts to RMS Titanic, Inc. (RMST). In October, Telly Savalas hosts a live television program featuring the opening of a suitcase recovered from *Titanic*'s debris field. Instead of riches, the valise holds a small amount of coins, jewelry, and banknotes, including Italian lire.

> *Titanic* survivor Eva Hart . . . labels the salvors 'fortune hunters, vultures, pirates.'

1992. Rival salvage company Marex Titanic Inc., which says it found the ship, sues in the Eastern District of Virginia for salvage rights and ownership of the 1,800 artifacts recovered by Titanic Ventures. The court, asserting jurisdiction over a non-U.S. ship in international waters in the interest of furthering international order, rejects Marex's claim in favor of Titanic Ventures. The decision is reversed on appeal because of a procedural technicality. Marex, which never recovered artifacts from the site and thus establish "possession," fades from the scene.

1993. In July, RMST recovers 800 artifacts. It files an action to seek exclusive salvage rights; on August 27, the Norfolk court issues a temporary warrant appointing RMST custodian of the wreck, site, and artifacts, pending possible claims from other parties. RMST settles with the Liverpool and London Steamship Protection and Indemnity Association, one of *Titanic*'s original insurers.

The wealth of artifacts from the *Titanic* wreck has motivated a number of corporate concerns to fight over access and rights to the ship's remains. (© **Alain Benainous/Gamma-Rapho via Getty Images.**)

1994. On June 7, the court names RMST salvor-in-possession of the *Titanic* and sole owner of any items recovered from the site. RMST's status as exclusive salvor is valid so long as it remains "in possession," a condition that effectively compels it to mount salvage expeditions every year or two. In July, more than 1,000 objects are recovered from the wreck site. In October, an exhibit of *Titanic* artifacts recovered by RMST opens at the National Maritime Museum in Greenwich, England.

International Groups Challenge RMST

1995. After learning about RMST's salvage efforts, the United States, United Kingdom, France, and Canada initiate discussions on a *Titanic* agreement.

1996. In February, John A. Josyln, an independent salvor, files a motion challenging RMST's standing as exclusive salvor of *Titanic* and declares his intention to visit and photograph the site. The court issues a preliminary injunction preventing him from searching, surveying, salvaging, or photographing the site. In August, the court enjoins third parties from entering the site to photograph it. The 1996 RMST expedition, in cooperation with The Discovery Channel and accompanied by a tourist cruise chartered to observe the recovery, nets 74 objects, but a highly publicized effort to raise a 20-ton piece of the hull fails. The company that arranged for the cruise—and provided funding and equipment for the expedition—later sues RMST, claiming co-salvor status and seeking $8 million for breach of contract, fraud, and other damages.

1997. *Titanic* exhibitions open in Memphis, St. Petersburg, Long Beach, Norfolk, and Hamburg, Germany. In April, The Discovery Channel airs *Titanic: Anatomy of A Disaster.* Negotiations on a *Titanic* agreement take place between 1997 and 2000 by the United States, United Kingdom, Canada, and France. In December, Paramount Pictures releases the film *Titanic*, including footage made during 12 dives to the site by director James Cameron.

1998. Deep Ocean Expeditions advertises "Operation *Titanic*." For $32,500, individuals are promised they will be able to visit and photograph the site in Russian deep-sea submersibles. RMST requests a preliminary injunction, and, in an order dated June 23, the court declares that RMST, as salvor-in-possession, has the right to exclude others from visiting the site in order to photograph it. In August, RMST completes another salvage expedition, again in conjunction with The Discovery Channel, and recovers 70 artifacts, including the piece of the hull it attempted to raise in 1996. Despite the court injunction, Operation *Titanic* visits the wreck site in September. Exhibitions are held in Boston and Japan.

1999. On March 24, the Fourth Circuit court reverses the earlier ruling, stating that RMST cannot exclude others from visiting, viewing, or photographing the *Titanic* site. RMST appeals to the Supreme Court; in October, the high court declines to review the case, leaving RMST without exclusive photographic rights. Exhibitions are held in St. Paul and Atlantic City. In November, shareholders vote to remove RMST president George Tulloch and the company's attorney, Allan Carlin. The new president, Arnie Geller, promises to accelerate the pace of artifact recovery. Tulloch and Carlin sue RMST seeking to reverse their removal.

Rules for Management of the Wreck Site

2000. In January, RMST settles with Tulloch and Carlin, paying the former executives $2.5 million in return for their promise not to meddle in company management for 18 months. Also in January, the United States, United Kingdom, Canada, and France develop a draft agreement concerning *Titanic*. The agreement sets forth rules for the management of the site, establishing in situ preservation as the preferred policy for the site. In April, RMST sues to prevent the U.S. from seeking an international agreement, arguing that such efforts are unconstitutional. In June, the National Oceanic and Atmospheric Administration (NOAA) requests public comments on proposed site-management guidelines.

> The primary goals of the salvage . . . remain decidedly nonarchaeological.

RMST announces plans for the summer's expedition; for the first time, the company intends to enter the ship to search for "high profile targets," including a $300-million diamond shipment. Also for the first time since salvage began in 1987, RMST hires a "project archaeologist." But the primary goals of the salvage—to maintain the project's salvor-in-possession status and recover "desirable objects" for display—remain decidedly non-archaeological.

On July 28, U.S. District Judge J. Calvitt Clarke issues an order forbidding RMST from penetrating or cutting into *Titanic* or from selling artifacts. The salvage expedition, conducted in August under the direction of CEO G. Michael Harris, is plagued by bad weather and equipment failures. Harris is fired at its conclusion. Following RMST's salvage operations, Zegrahm Expeditions, a Seattle-based company, takes a small group of adventure tourists to the *Titanic* site.

On September 15, Judge Clarke dismisses RMST's case against NOAA and the Department of State, which had been negotiating an international agreement on the *Titanic*. The judge notes that RMST's claims were premature, but that RMST could renew its motion if and when an agreement was signed and implemented.

Editor's Note

The ownership of artifacts and wreck site status were not settled in the courts until 2011.

Titanic Should Be Left Undisturbed

Paul Lee

The following viewpoint describes the status of the *Titanic* wreck as of 2010. The author explains that after two decades of expeditions and artifact recovery, *Titanic* was left relatively undisturbed for almost ten years. Data and images from a planned 2010 expedition, he writes, might help scientists quantify how much of the wreck's decay is natural and how much is caused by human intervention. He is skeptical that the degradation of the hull is due to the increased growth of rusticles—icicle-like colonies of bacteria or other microorganisms—and laments the fact that expeditions have focused on documentaries and commercial ventures instead of scientific research. Paul Lee is the author of *The* Titanic *and the Indifferent Stranger: The Complete Story of the* Titanic *and the* Californian. He has a doctorate in nuclear physics from York University and is based in Cambridge, England.

SOURCE. Paul Lee, "The *Titanic*, 2005 to 2010," paullee.com.

From the moment the wreck was found, the *Titanic* had endured 20 years of intrusive visits, whether for research, salvage, or just plain greed and publicity; trips occurred in 1985, 1986, 1987, 1991, 1993, 1994, 1995, 1996, 1998, 2000, 2001, 2002 (including an illegal plundering of artefacts), 2003, 2004 and finally 2005. Then, they stopped. When the [Russian scientific research vessel R/V *Akademik Mstislav*] *Keldysh* and its two Mir submersibles left the wreck co-ordinates in 2005, those on board were the last to view the ship for five years. There was talk of commercial trips to the wreck in 2006 and 2007 . . . but these never came to fruition as the Russian government seconded the Mirs [deep-submergence vehicles] to Lake Baikal and to help in oil pipe inspection tasks.

In 2010, the hiatus finished. The salvors of artefacts from the wreck, RMS Titanic, Inc. [RMST], announced a trip to the *Titanic*'s hulk not for salvage, but to chronicle the rusted remains, and to have these findings made available to the world. Oh, and to help in a 2012 History Channel documentary [*Titanic at 100: Mystery Solved*] too.

It seemed intriguing. Visits to the wreck had been so frequent it was hard to deduce what damage and degredation had been caused by human visitors or natural corrosion. With no visitors to the wreck in five years, we had a chance to identify what Mother Nature had done to the wreck, and what human intervention had inflicted. Dr. [Robert D.] Ballard, in his *National Geographic* tirade in 2004, placed the blame for the ship's deterioration on human curiosity. His article included a diagram . . . which showed a sad prediction for the *Titanic*'s condition in forthcoming years [2012 and 2112].

> We had a chance to identify what Mother Nature had done to the wreck, and what human intervention had inflicted.

Titanic Is Granted UNESCO Protection

The United Nations has moved to protect the wreck of the *Titanic* amid growing concern at its deterioration as a result of tourist visits and exploration submarines crashing into its structure.

The 100-year-old wreck has been brought under the cover of the 2001 UNESCO convention on the protection of underwater cultural heritage, which gives signed-up member states the right to prevent exploration deemed unscientific or unethical, seize illicitly recovered artifacts and close their ports to all vessels undertaking exploration that is not done according to the principles of the doctrine. . . . The protections are limited by the fact that neither the US nor Canada is among the 41 signatory states and a number of the tourist and exploration trips chartered to the wreck site 4,000m [13,123 feet or about 2.5 miles] under the sea off the coast of Newfoundland come from those countries.

SOURCE. *Robert Booth, "*Titanic *Wreck to Be Protected by UN Maritime Convention,"* The Guardian *(UK), April 5, 2012. www.theguardian.com/uk/2012/apr/05/titanic-wreck-protected-un-convention.*

Fortunately, although we are still a year away from comparing the wreck with the 2012 artist's diagram, we are confident that the prediction is alarmist.

Natural vs. Man-Made Damage to the Wreck Site

Others seemed to agree with Ballard; Jack Eaton and Charles Haas [authors and trustees of the Titanic International Society] alleged that the marks of manipulator arms could be seen on some areas of the wreck, for instance, the captain's bathroom, to pry the walls apart for better imaging. But their words should be treated with caution: in the second edition of *Titanic: Triumph and Tragedy* they present two photographs of the buckled starboard bow under the well deck, one from 1987 and the other from 1993; they write that "[the second photograph] shows corrosion has softened the contours of the shell plating's exposed edge, suggesting that disintegration of the ship's hull is accelerating." This is actually slightly dishonest; the photographs are shot from slightly different locations, and the second one (1993) seems to be out of focus. Then there is the issue of colour: the first picture has a ghostly blue tint, like most of the 1987 photos this author has seen, whereas the one 6 years later shows the rust colouring of the hull very well.

But others disagreed with this. Ballard's ghost-written tome of 1987 [*The Discovery of the Titanic*, co-written by Rick Archbold] mentions that bacteria are responsible for the long iron tendrils called "rusticles" and later analysis by Dr. Roy Cullimore and Dr. Lori Johnston [Canadian scientists] have added to our knowledge of which bacteria are causing the deterioration. Indeed, Johnston even told UK TV presenter Tony Robinson that 200 lbs of iron were being "eaten" each day. In 5 years, this amounts to 365,000 lbs (166 tonnes) . . . and in 98 years this equals 7.2 million lbs (3300 metric tonnes); a lot, but far short of the actual mass of the *Titanic* herself. These two microbiologists have written a paper; it mentions "at least [a] 30%" increase in rusticle formation between 1996 and 1998, and that the upper promenade deck (boat deck?) is deteriorating "from the aft" moving forwards at a rate of approximately 30cm a year. They expect the deck structure of [the] wreck to have gone by 2028, but concede that "other elements of the ship will stay intact for hundreds of years."

But there was one dissenter; Dr. Tim Foecke; in his co-authored book *What Really Sank the Titanic?* he dismisses the rusticle argument on the grounds that the mechanism for the digestion of iron had never been described. However, in 2010, it was announced that a brand new bacteria had been cultivated from samples gathered during the 1991 IMAX voyage: *Halomonas titanicae.*

Some have claimed that the "increased" rusticle growth between, say, the 1987 and 1991 expedition are indications of an increase in the degredation of the hull. This author is sceptical. The rusticle structures are so flimsy that they disintegrate in the wash from a submersible's propellor . . . not to mention the undersea currents which have been reported to be quite strong at times. Unless one can definitely associate a rusticle in one photograph with a rusticle taken years later, it seems silly to definitely state the amount of deterioration in the meantime. If anything, rusticles inside the hull, and protected from undersea currents, would give a better indication of their growth, but we must be careful on this issue as silt and mud can be carried far inside the ship by the currents and dislodge the fragile rusticles.

> "Nothing like the amount of material anticipated has been released [by RMST]."

Difficulties Obtaining New Data

At any rate, the Research Vessel the *Jean Charcot* was ready to take its assemblage of scientists, technicians, historians, TV personnel and so on to the wreck site in August 2010 to catalogue the *Titanic* in 3D images and sonar data. The mission was a collaboration between RMS Titanic, Inc., the Woods Hole Oceanographic Institution (who had participated in the initial discovery of the wreck in 1985), the Waitt Institute for Discovery, the Institute of Nautical Archaeology and the History Channel.

One very early release of material was a sonar view of the bow section. It showed that the foremast, which had become fractured into an L-shape about 2004, was still in place. I had thought that it had long ago snapped and fallen either off the ship or into one of the nearby cavernous cargo holds. I was pleased to have been proven

On the wreck of *Titanic*, rusticles cover all surfaces of what was once a first-class cabin. (© **Emory Kristof/ National Geographic/ Getty Images.**)

wrong. Inspection of the remainder of the image showed no massive signs of collapse in 5 years.

But then . . . the aims of the expedition became unravelled thanks to the efforts of Hurricane Danielle and Earl, and then Igor. The *Jean Charcot* scurried back to port and sat impotently there for days and days before a safe window of opportunity emerged and the vessel made its way back to the wreck.

Obviously keeping the prime of material back for itself and its 2012 documentary, I have felt as though *Titanic* enthusiasts have been treated like hungry dogs while a complacent master [RMST] throws scraps to his ravenous, baying pets. Certainly, nothing like the amount of material anticipated has been released. Even when the *Jean Charcot* was in port, the images we obtained were scant. In 1986, images from the wreck were beamed back to shore and shown on television that very same day, and this was with technology comparatively primitive to the equipment available in 2010. . . . My attempts to engage RMS Titanic, Inc. both before and after the 2010 mission have been in vain: messages to the one email address that is provided (in mass mail-outs to hawk their wares) gets bounced back, their Facebook page provides no contact information, and even their company website is lacking in information to get in touch, either by email or by post.

VIEWPOINT 5

Ship Designers Have Not Learned the Right Lessons from the *Titanic* Disaster

Edward Tenner

In 2013, a few months before the hundredth anniversary of the *Titanic* disaster, a cruise ship ran aground off the western coast of Italy, killing thirty-two passengers. The author of the following viewpoint uses the two maritime disasters as examples of the theory of "conservation of catastrophe" as described by historian William H. McNeill. While newer ships benefit from reforms adopted after the 1912 disaster and other technological advances, the features that make them safer also lead to complacency and obscure other risks, the author explains. This phenomenon is also evident in other areas of design and engineering, such as tall buildings and dams. According to the author, the lessons adopted from disasters like *Titanic* are no substitute for vigilance. Edward Tenner is a former college

---

SOURCE. Edward Tenner, "A Model Disaster," *Popular Science*, April 17, 2012.

teacher and executive editor in book publishing who writes about society and technology. He is the author of *Our Own Devices: How Technology Remakes Humanity*.

The hundredth anniversary of the wreck of the *Titanic* on April 15 [2012] provides a welcome moment to celebrate the many great strides made by engineers. In 2012, people move around the world more quickly and more safely than ever before. But the fate of the *Costa Concordia*, the cruise ship that ran aground off the coast of western Italy in January, reminds us that no matter how much progress we make, disasters still happen. It also presents a question: After a century of advances in naval engineering, why are we still unable to prevent deadly wrecks?

My graduate-school teacher, William H. McNeill, explored a similar question in a 1989 essay, "Control and Catastrophe in Human Affairs." McNeill had eco-

Safety and technology improvements did not prevent the *Costa Concordia* disaster. The massive cruise ship ran aground off the coast of Italy in 2012, killing thirty-two passengers. (© **Laura Lezza/Getty Images.**)

nomic wrecks, not shipwrecks, in mind. At the time he was writing, regulators were confronting the savings and loan crisis, which itself was just the latest in a long series of financial and monetary debacles dating back to at least the Panic of 1873. Why were regulators unable to better manage the system? After each panic or crash, they would step in with reforms, yet no matter how careful the design, at some point those reforms would fail, and catastrophe would return anew. McNeill proposed that the problem was not poorly designed reforms, but rather reforms that worked all too well. They achieved their intended purpose, but they did so by shifting risk to less-organized places. "It certainly seems as though every gain in precision in the coordination of human activity and every heightening of efficiency in production were matched by a new vulnerability to breakdown," McNeill concluded. "If this is really the case, then the conservation of catastrophe may indeed be a law of nature like the conservation of energy."

The Theory of Conservation of Catastrophe

We can observe another variation of the conservation of catastrophe in the construction of medieval cathedrals. When builders discovered clever ways to construct larger and airier, more light-filled testaments to the glory of God, they incorporated them enthusiastically. Those new levels of achievement, though, also exposed the structures to previously unknown hazards. For instance, when the architects of the Cathedral of Saint Peter in Beauvais, France, set out to build the tallest church in history, they deployed the then cutting-edge technology of flying buttresses. The lightweight buttresses were a brilliant innovation, but the soaring design they enabled also revealed previously irrelevant structural flaws, still under scholarly investigation, that led to a partial collapse of the choir in a windstorm in 1284, a dozen years after construction was complete. (High winds also doomed another landmark, the Tacoma Narrows Bridge in Washington, six centuries later.)

Disaster may also reassert itself when engineers are so successful that they actually transform the environment. In attempting to control flooding on the Mississippi River, for instance, engineers built levees close to the riverbanks. Floodwaters that were once dispersed across a wide plain were now confined to a high, narrow channel. It worked well for the most part—but narrow waters run faster, so when the levees were breached or overtopped, as was inevitable, the same volume now spread more quickly, causing greater damage. Similarly, forest managers' increasing ability to suppress wildfires can lead to the buildup of brush—which turns out to be a far more powerful fuel for the fires that do eventually rage out of control.

"The size and complexity that make new ships so impressive may exacerbate trouble when disaster does strike."

We can see the same three trends at work in marine disasters: First, genuinely safer systems can sometimes cause the crew to miscalculate risk. Second, genuinely better engineering can expose previously unrealized weak points. And third, the size and complexity that make new ships so impressive may exacerbate trouble when disaster does strike.

The *Titanic* demonstrated all three effects spectacularly, and precisely because its designers and officers were some of the most capable and experienced men of their professions. Captain Edward Smith's declaration in 1907 that "I cannot imagine any condition which could cause a ship to founder" might sound tragically foolhardy today, but he had reason to be confident. Big iron and steel ships really had held their own against icebergs—that same year, the *Kronprinz Wilhelm*, a German superliner, had survived such a collision with only minor damage. But the new transatlantic steamers were no more stable than their weakest points. The *Titanic*'s rivets and steel plating, analysis of samples from late-20th-century dives has suggested, may have failed in the collision. Furthermore, the scale of the ship, far from being protective as the designers and captain believed, made the hazard even greater. Forensic naval architect Philip Sims noted recently that the *Titanic* was three times as large as the iceberg-surviving *Kronprinz Wilhelm* and was "moving 30 percent faster, so it had five times the impact energy pushing in her side plates." And in the event of the disaster, that size only made matters worse. The length of passageways delayed some passengers in reaching the lifeboats, many of which were launched half-empty.

The disaster of the *Titanic* led to reforms. Congress began requiring ships to monitor the airwaves at all times. The International Convention for the Safety of Life at Sea in 1913 called for ships to carry enough lifeboats to hold every passenger, and for the creation of an International Ice Patrol, to monitor icebergs. Yet disaster just as surely reasserted itself. The addition of lifeboats made some vessels less stable; the excursion ship *Eastland*, already relatively top-heavy before the installation of additional post-*Titanic* lifeboats, capsized in Chicago Harbor in 1915, killing 844 passengers. The ship was overloaded, and the alarmed crowd rushed from side to side until it listed fatally.

Repeating Errors of Overconfidence

The operators of the *Costa Concordia* appear to have repeated some of the same errors. The cruise-ship industry trumpeted the safety record of its shallow-draft megaships, originating in the 1980s. They became as iconic in the age of mass tourism as the transatlantic liners had been in the heyday of American immigration.

With 4,200 passengers and crew, the *Costa Concordia* was far from the largest of its kind. Its captain was also experienced and well regarded by his peers. But as with the *Titanic*, the long period of success may have been misinterpreted. Some witnesses claim that the captain was distracted by conversations with passengers on the bridge at the moment of impact. He may have been overly confident because he had navigated the ship successfully on a similar maneuver only months earlier. Like Captain Smith, he has been criticized for delaying evacuation, too—possibly overly confident in the ship's resilience—thereby losing an hour before the ship began to list, which rendered half the lifeboats useless.

We don't yet have evidence regarding the *Costa Concordia*'s hull and whether the construction may have had weaknesses revealed only under unusual stress, as at Beauvais and on the *Titanic*. But it's very possible that construction of the hull did not assume that rocks could inflict a gash 160 feet long. We'll know more when the designers and builders testify.

> Engineers should remain aware, though, that new designs can bring about new disasters.

Finally, the *Costa Concordia*'s scale, like the *Titanic*'s, created unforeseen problems. Now as then, the ship's evacuation routes confused many passengers. The *Costa Concordia*'s designers may have thought that by using advanced evacuation dynamics software to plan the interior, they could assure an orderly exit even from the most remote quarters. But Dracos Vassalos, a professor of maritime safety at the University of Strathclyde in Scotland, recently noted in *USA Today* that "the internal architecture of cruise ships is so complex that even with the same effects being accounted for in . . . experiments, computer simulations or, indeed, in real-life accidents, we could potentially see a different outcome every time we simulate the accident."

The Need to Remain Vigilant

Engineers should, of course, continue to develop measures to prevent disasters. Collision-resistant construction, however imperfect, has helped save thousands of lives. On the *Titanic*, it bought hours of precious time; if evacuation had been ordered earlier and the nearby *Californian* had responded to distress calls promptly, the death toll might have been much lower. And the great majority of *Costa Concordia* passengers were rescued without serious injury.

Engineers should remain aware, though, that new designs can bring about new disasters—or, as McNeill concluded, "Both intelligence and catastrophe appear to move in a world of unlimited permutation and combination, provoking an open-ended sequence of challenge and response." Debates about the *Titanic*'s end continue, and hearings and legal proceedings regarding the *Costa Concordia* will probably also take years. But wherever the fault lies, we have already been reminded that there is no substitute for vigilance, imagination and enlightened paranoia. In the words of Lewis Carroll's Red Queen, we need to run as fast as we can to stay where we are.

VIEWPOINT 6

Titanic Sank Because of Weak, Poorly Made Rivets

William J. Broad

The following viewpoint reports that researchers have determined that low-quality rivets and an overburdened company are key reasons for *Titanic*'s sinking. Over a decade, a group of researchers reviewed archives from the company that built *Titanic* and examined rivets recovered from the wreck. They discovered that although the ship had every conceivable luxury, the shipbuilders used low-quality rivets because of a rivet shortage. According to the researchers, the company was overwhelmed by the simultaneous construction of the world's three largest ships: *Olympic*, *Titanic*, and *Britannic*. William J. Broad is a science journalist and the author of eight books. He is a senior writer at the *New York Times*.

SOURCE. William J. Broad, "In Weak Rivets, a Possible Key to *Titanic*'s Doom," *New York Times*, April 15, 2008.

Researchers have discovered that the builder of the *Titanic* struggled for years to obtain enough good rivets and riveters and ultimately settled on faulty materials that doomed the ship, which sank 96 years ago Tuesday.

The builder's own archives, two scientists say, harbor evidence of a deadly mix of low quality rivets and lofty ambition as the builder labored to construct the three biggest ships in the world at once—the *Titanic* and two sisters, the *Olympic* and the *Britannic*.

For a decade, the scientists have argued that the storied liner went down fast after hitting an iceberg because the ship's builder used substandard rivets that popped their heads and let tons of icy seawater rush in. More than 1,500 people died.

When the safety of the rivets was first questioned 10 years ago, the builder ignored the accusation and said it did not have an archivist who could address the issue.

Now, historians say new evidence uncovered in the archive of the builder, Harland and Wolff, in Belfast, Northern Ireland, settles the argument and finally solves the riddle of one of the most famous sinkings of all time. The company says the findings are deeply flawed.

Historical Research on Rivet Shortage

Each of the great ships under construction required three million rivets that acted like glue to hold everything together. In a new book, the scientists say the shortages peaked during the *Titanic*'s construction.

"The board was in crisis mode," one of the authors, Jennifer Hooper McCarty, who studied the archives, said in an interview. "It was constant stress. Every meeting it was, 'There's problems with the rivets and we need to hire more people.'"

Apart from the archives, the team gleaned clues from 48 rivets recovered from the hulk of the *Titanic*, modern tests and computer simulations. They also compared metal from the *Titanic* with other metals from the same era, and looked at documentation about what engineers and shipbuilders of that era considered state of the art.

The scientists say the troubles began when its ambitious building plans forced Harland and Wolff to reach beyond its usual suppliers of rivet iron and include smaller forges, as disclosed in company and British government papers. Small forges tended to have less skill and experience.

> So the liner [*Titanic*] . . . in at least one instance relied on cheaper materials.

Adding to the problem, in buying iron for the *Titanic*'s rivets, the company ordered No. 3 bar, known as "best"—not No. 4, known as "best-best," the scientists found. Shipbuilders of the day typically used No. 4 iron for anchors, chains and rivets, they discovered.

So the liner, whose name was meant to be synonymous with opulence, in at least one instance relied on cheaper materials.

Many of the rivets studied by the scientists—recovered from the *Titanic*'s resting place two miles down in the North Atlantic by divers over two decades—were found to be riddled with high concentrations of slag. A glassy residue of smelting, slag can make rivets brittle and prone to fracture.

"Some material the company bought was not rivet quality," said the other author of the book, Timothy Foecke of the National Institute of Standards and Technology, a federal agency in Gaithersburg, Md.

The company also faced shortages of skilled riveters, the archives showed. Dr. McCarty said that for a half year, from late 1911 to April 1912, when the *Titanic* set sail, the company's board discussed the problem at every meeting. For instance, on Oct. 28, 1911, Lord William Pirrie, the company's chairman, expressed concern over the lack of riveters and called for new hiring efforts.

Metallurgical Research on *Titanic*'s Rivets

In their research, the scientists, who are metallurgists, found that good riveting took great skill. The iron had to be heated to a precise cherry red color and beaten by the right combination of hammer blows. Mediocre work could hide problems.

"Hand riveting was tricky," said Dr. McCarty, whose doctoral thesis at Johns Hopkins University analyzed the *Titanic*'s rivets.

Steel beckoned as a solution. Shipbuilders of the day were moving from iron to steel rivets, which were stronger. And machines could install them, improving workmanship.

The rival Cunard line, the scientists found, had switched to steel rivets years before, using them, for instance, throughout the *Lusitania*.

The scientists discovered that Harland and Wolff also used steel rivets—but only on the *Titanic*'s central hull,

A piece of *Titanic*'s hull recovered from the wreck site and on display in Chicago in 2000 shows the rivets that held together the iron pieces. (© Tannen Maury/AFP/Getty Images.)

where stresses were expected to be greatest. Iron rivets were chosen for the stern and bow.

And the bow, as fate would have it, is where the iceberg struck. Studies of the wreck show that six seams opened up in the ship's bow plates. And the damage, Dr. Foecke noted, "ends close to where the rivets transition from iron to steel."

The scientists argue that better rivets would have probably kept the *Titanic* afloat long enough for rescuers to arrive before the icy plunge, saving hundreds of lives.

The researchers make their case, and detail their archive findings, in *What Really Sank the Titanic* (Citadel Press).

Shipbuilders Challenge the Findings

Reactions run from anger to admiration. James Alexander Carlisle, whose grandfather was a *Titanic* riveter, has bluntly denounced the rivet theory on his Web site. "No way!" Mr. Carlisle writes.

> Reactions [to the rivets research findings] run from anger to admiration.

For its part, Harland and Wolff, after its long silence, now rejects the charge. "There was nothing wrong with the materials," Joris Minne, a company spokesman, said last week. Mr. Minne noted that one of the sister ships, the *Olympic*, sailed without incident for 24 years, until retirement. (The *Britannic* sank in 1916 after hitting a mine.)

David Livingstone, a former Harland and Wolff official, called the book's main points misleading. Mr. Livingstone said big shipyards often had to scramble. On a recent job, he noted, Harland and Wolff had to look to Romania to find welders.

Mr. Livingstone also called the slag evidence painfully circumstantial, saying no real proof linked the hull opening to bad rivets. "It's only waffle," he said of the team's arguments.

But a naval historian praised the book as solving a mystery that has baffled investigators for nearly a century.

"It's fascinating," said Tim Trower, who reviews books for the Titanic Historical Society, a private group in Indian Orchard, Mass. "This puts in the final nail in the arguments and explains why the incident was so dramatically bad."

The Irony of the Flawed Rivets

The *Titanic* had every conceivable luxury: cafes, squash courts, a swimming pool, Turkish baths, a barbershop and three libraries. Its owners also bragged about its safety. In a brochure, the White Star Line described the ship as "designed to be unsinkable."

On her inaugural voyage, on the night of April 14, 1912, the ship hit the iceberg around 11:40 PM and sank in a little more than two and a half hours. Most everyone assumed the iceberg had torn a huge gash in the starboard hull.

The discovery in 1985 of the *Titanic* wreck began many new inquiries. In 1996, an expedition found, beneath obscuring mud, not a large gash but six narrow slits where bow plates appeared to have parted. Naval experts suspected that rivets had popped along the seams, letting seawater rush in under high pressure.

A specialist in metal fracture, Dr. Foecke got involved in 1997, analyzing two salvaged rivets. He was astonished to find about three times more slag than occurs in modern wrought iron.

In early 1998, he and a team of marine forensic experts announced their rivet findings, calling them tentative.

A Riddle Solved

Dr. Foecke, in addition to working at the National Institute of Standards and Technology, also taught and lectured part time at Johns Hopkins. There he met Dr. McCarty, who got hooked on the riddle, as did her thesis adviser.

The team acquired rivets from salvors who pulled up hundreds of artifacts from the sunken liner. The scientists also collected old iron of the era—including some from the Brooklyn Bridge—to make comparisons. The new work seemed only to bolster the bad-rivet theory.

In 2003, after graduating from Johns Hopkins, Dr. McCarty traveled to England and located the Harland and Wolff archives at the Public Record Office of Northern Ireland, in Belfast.

> [White Star Line was] stretched to the limit as it struggled to build the world's three biggest ships simultaneously.

She also explored the archives of the British Board of Trade, which regulated shipping and set material standards, and of Lloyd's of London, which set shipbuilding standards. And she worked at Oxford University and obtained access to its libraries.

What emerged was a picture of a company stretched to the limit as it struggled to build the world's three biggest ships simultaneously. Dr. McCarty also found evidence of complacency. For instance, the Board of Trade gave up testing iron for shipbuilding in 1901 because it saw iron metallurgy as a mature field, unlike the burgeoning world of steel.

Dr. McCarty said she enjoyed telling middle and high school students about the decade of rivet forensics, as well as the revelations from the British archives.

"They get really excited," she said. "That's why I love the story. People see it and get mesmerized."

Titanic's Wireless Operators Withheld Information for Profit

New York Herald

In an article from 1912, a newspaper reports allegations that *Titanic*'s wireless operators were advised to withhold information in order to sell their stories. In the following viewpoint, the authors write that the wireless company's chief engineer admitted to the scheme and felt that efforts to get the highest price for the operators' stories were justified. In addition, further inquiries were likely because the operators also were accused of ignoring messages sent by US president William Howard Taft inquiring about an aide on the ship. (Note: After the original publication of this viewpoint, testimony revealed the *New York Times* paid $500 to the surviving wireless operator for exclusive rights to his story.) The *New York Herald* was a daily newspaper known for sensationalistic reporting that was published from 1835 to 1924 and at one point had the highest circulation in the country.

SOURCE. "'Keep Your Mouth Shut; Big Money for You,' Was Message to Hide News," *New York Herald*, April 21, 1912. Reproduced by permission.

While the world was waiting three days for information concerning the fate of the *Titanic*, for part of the time at least, details concerning the disaster were being withheld by the wireless operator of the steamship *Carpathia* under specific orders from T.W. Sammis, chief engineer of the Marconi Wireless Company of America, who had arranged the sale of the story.

This was admitted yesterday [April 20, 2012] by Mr. Sammis, who defended his action. He said he was justified for getting for the wireless operators the largest amount he could for the details of the sinking of the ship, the rescue of the passengers and the other information the world had waited for.

The first information concerning the loss of the *Titanic* came Monday evening, and it was known at that time the survivors were on board the *Carpathia*. About midnight the first of the list of survivors began to come by wireless, and from that time until Thursday night, when the rescue ship arrived in port, the world waited and waited in vain for the details of how the "unsinkable ship" had gone down.

> 'If you are wise, hold story. The Marconi company will take care of you.'

Three messages were sent to the *Carpathia* telling the operator to send out no news concerning the disaster. Two of these were unsigned, and the last one had the signature of Mr. Sammis.

"Keep Mouth Shut; Big Money"

The first message was unsigned, and it is said it was sent as a list of names of survivors were being forwarded. It read: "Keep your mouth shut. Hold story. Big money for you."

The messages from the *Carpathia* to the Marconi office concerning this matter were not available, but there

was evidently some communication, for the second unsigned message followed after an interval. This message read: "If you are wise, hold story. The Marconi company will take care of you."

An injured Harold Bride (center), the sole surviving wireless operator of *Titanic*, is helped off the *Carpathia*. The *New York Times* paid Bride for exclusive rights to his story. (**© World History Archive/Alamy.**)

The third and last message was addressed to "Marconi officer, the *Carpathia* and the *Titanic*," and signed "S.M. Sammis," chief engineer of the Marconi Company of America. This one read: "Stop. Say nothing. Hold your story for dollars in four figures. Mr. Marconi agreeing. Will meet you at dock."

Mr. Sammis was at the Waldorf-Astoria yesterday at the hearing before the sub-committee of the United States Senate, and he was asked about the message.

A Defiant Response at the Hearing

"It is reported," he was told, "that a message was sent by you to the wireless operator on the *Carpathia* to which you gave the orders or at least said to him not to give out any details of the sinking of the *Titanic*, as you had arranged for four figures."

"Well?" he said is a defiant way.

"Did you send such a message?"

"Maybe. What of it?" he replied.

"It would be interesting to know if you actually sent such a message."

"Yes, I sent the message, but whose business is it?" Mr. Sammis asked with some heat.

"Perhaps it was no one's business," he was told, "but it is interesting to know that when the world was horror stricken over the disaster and waiting for the news, that there were persons preparing to capitalize [on] the suspense and had arranged for 'four figures.'"

> The chief engineer of the [Marconi] company was marketing the information of the disaster.

"Do you blame me for this," retorted Mr. Sammis, as he backed up against the wall. "Do you blame me for getting the highest price I could for the operator for the story he had to tell about the collision and the rescue. I thought I was doing a good turn for him, and I can't see how it is the business of anyone."

Further Inquiries Likely

It is not unlikely that the sending of these messages with the apparent result that no details of the disaster came from the relief ship will form part of the inquiry that is being made by a sub-committee of the Senate. Part of this inquiry has been directed as to why a message from President [William Howard] Taft asking for information about Major Archibald W. Butt was unanswered, and it is not unlikely that in view of the message from Mr. Sammis that this will be taken up again.

While these messages were intercepted by more than one wireless receiving station, there is one place where the Senate Committee could undoubtedly get copies of them. The New York Navy Yard has a powerful receiving station, and has what is known as an "intercepted message" book. These messages are considered confidential and are never given out, but the book would undoubtedly be at the disposal of the investigating committee.

Senator Smith said yesterday that the authorities in Washington knew on Thursday long before the *Carpathia* arrived, that the White Star line was contemplating the return of part of the *Titanic* crew to England by the steamship *Cedric*, and this information undoubtedly came from a government station.

John W. Griggs, one time Attorney General of the United States and Governor of New Jersey, is president of the Marconi Wireless Company of America. He said last night he had not heard that the chief engineer of the company was marketing the information of the disaster.

"This is a matter which will be looked into," he said. "I know nothing about it, had not heard of it before, and, of course, cannot say what will be done until it is brought to my attention in an official way."

VIEWPOINT 8

The Passenger Evacuation on *Titanic* Reflected the Stark Class Divisions of the Time

Frank Whelan

In this viewpoint, a newspaper columnist uses a 1912 letter by a prominent Pennsylvanian to discuss the stark divisions between the social classes in the early twentieth century. The *Titanic* disaster, the author explains, illustrates how the lives of richer passengers were valued more than the lives of poor passengers. Although third-class passengers were responsible for most of the revenue on transatlantic ships, they were thought of as an unruly mob. Because of this prejudiced attitude, steerage passengers were locked away from first-class areas on *Titanic*, and many were denied access to the deck with the lifeboats in time to be saved. Frank Whelan is a reporter for the *Morning Call*, a newspaper in Pennsylvania's Lehigh Valley, and has been

---

SOURCE. Frank Whelan, "Archives Reveal That *Titanic* Depicts Class Tensions Accurately," *Morning Call*, January 14, 1998.

writing a history column for almost thirty years. He is the author of *Lehigh County: A Bicentennial Look Back at an American Community*.

In the early 20th century, when Tilghman S. Cooper of Coopersburg spoke, people in the Lehigh Valley listened.

A member of the family that gave its name to the borough, he was the leading Jersey cattle breeder in America. Cattle sales at Cooper's Linden Grove Farm attracted breeders from around the world. To study the breed, he had traveled to every known corner of the globe. So, when Cooper wrote a letter to the editor of the *Morning Call* on April 22, 1912 about the sinking of the White Star liner *Titanic*, the newspaper gave it a separate column on page 4.

Cooper began by saying he had crossed the Atlantic often. "I have sailed on such steamers as the *Lusitania*, *Mauretania*, *Baltic*, *Kaiser Wilhelm Der Grosse*, *Oceanic*, *Majestic* and *Britannia* and years ago on many others not so noted," he wrote. He knew Captain E.J. Smith of the *Titanic* well. "It was my pleasure to cross with him several times on the *Oceanic* . . . He was not only a sea captain, but a gentleman of the first class order," Cooper wrote.

Valuing the Rich over the Poor

But Cooper's letter was about a larger subject. He had heard reports that many of the people saved from the *Titanic* were steerage passengers, the poor who traveled third class.

In his 40 years of travel, Cooper had often lain awake in his berth listening to the ship's fog horn and fearing a disaster that would turn the steerage passengers into an uncontrollable mob. It was well known, he said, that in a disaster "men of this class" would "refuse assistance to their fellow passengers, struggling nearby in the water,

Immigrants Were a Primary Source of Revenue for Transatlantic Passenger Ships

The White Star Line made the decision to build the three Olympic class ships for sound business reasons, not as an exercise in corporate vanity as has sometimes been suggested. Until the advent of air travel in the mid 20th Century, the only way to cross the Atlantic Ocean was by steamship, and it was an immensely profitable industry. Not only did businessmen have to travel back and forth between Europe and North America, but the rising tide of westward-bound immigrants represented an unprecedented source of income: by 1900 most of the operating revenue for these ships came from the fares paid by their immigrant passengers. Wealthy and titled passengers in First Class were nice to have, but the men and women in Third Class were the steamship lines' bread-and-butter. Hence, competition for that immigrant trade was fierce, particularly among the German and British lines. The advertising value of having the biggest, most luxurious, or fastest ship on the North Atlantic was a powerful draw to potential travelers.

SOURCE. *Daniel Allen Butler, "White Star Line Built the* Titanic *to Compete with* Lusitania, Mauretania, *"* Denver Post, *March 27, 2012.*

even beating the fingers of drowning women as they clutched the side of life boats." Cooper's answer to this problem was to ban steerage passengers from "high class ships like the *Titanic*."

Cooper was aware that some people would think him unfair. But how could one compare, he suggested, the loss of a steerage passenger to that of just two of the first class passengers lost on the Titanic.

[*Titanic* victims] George Widener, "who developed the traction system in Philadelphia from a toy to its present state of modern and efficient service," [and] "Mr. Charles M. Hays, recognized as a power in the Grand Trunk Railway system," said Cooper, were worth saving. "America cannot afford to lose such men."

> It was standard procedure for steerage to be separated from other parts of a ship by locked gates.

Cooper could not have known that the first reports were incorrect, that most of those saved were first-class, women and children, and that most of those who died were steerage men, women and children. But his letter brings up an issue that is still being argued 85 years later.

Doomed to Death Below Decks

In the general praise that has fallen on the new movie *Titanic*, some critics have been uncomfortable with the way first class passengers' treatment of third class passengers is depicted. One called it neo-Marxist. Another labeled it Dickensian. But in many ways the film accurately reflected the *Titanic* and the era of which it was a part.

It was standard procedure for steerage to be separated from other parts of a ship by locked gates. Following the collision with the iceberg, some of the *Titanic*'s staff tried to help third-class women and children to the lifeboats. But no real effort was made to find those in third class that might have been trapped and confused below. A high proportion of women and children in steerage were lost, including all the large families. And third-class men were denied access to the first class deck until most of the lifeboats were gone.

This class difference flew in the face of economic reality. In fact, if steamship lines like White Star had followed Cooper's advice and banned steerage, they would have cut themselves off from their major source of revenue. It was the thousands who sailed third class that paid the company back for their huge investments in ships like the *Titanic*.

In 1912, the newspapers were full of accounts of the heroism of first-class passengers on the *Titanic*. Every newspaper reader in the country learned how the brave Benjamin Guggenheim had put on his formal wear so he could die like a gentleman or how John Jacob Astor had placed his young wife in the lifeboat, helped load the other women and children and then went gallantly to his own death.

But in the mainstream press, steerage passengers were almost uniformly shown as an unruly mob of Italian and Slavic immigrants who were only kept under control by the guns of the brave Anglo-Saxon officers.

An elegant first-class parlor suite on *Titanic* was photographed before the ship's ill-fated maiden voyage. Passengers from different classes did not mix aboard the ship. (© **Popperfoto/ Getty Images.**)

The Social Realities of 1912

This view reflected the general attitude of the time. In most European countries, a neo-feudal class system was firmly in place. In the United States, the gap between rich and poor was huge. Anti-foreign and racist feelings were running at high tide. Lynchings of African-Americans north and south were common.

Labor struggles, most of them unsuccessful, were commonplace. Wages were low, children and adults worked long hours in conditions that would not be tolerated in Third World countries today. On March 25, 1911, 145 mostly women employees died in the fire at Triangle Shirtwaist Company in New York. And that was but one of many.

Even in 1912, there were people who hoped that something greater than a disaster would come out of the *Titanic* tragedy. Shortly after the sinking, an editorial cartoon appeared in the *New York Herald*, the *Morning Call* and other newspapers. It showed labor and capital being guided by a grim Uncle Sam who says, "My Brothers, the Rich and the Poor Have Died Together: Why Can't They Live Together?" It was a noble sentiment, but one that apparently had little impact in 1912. Eighty-five years later, in the era of gated communities, those differences, if no longer as extreme, remain with us.

VIEWPOINT 9

An Actress Who Survived the Disaster Began the Legend That Is *Titanic*

Robert Fulford

The following viewpoint discusses the contrasting ways in which *Titanic* has been used as a metaphor in popular culture. According to the author, the narrative tradition associated with the disaster began just twenty-nine days after survivors arrived in New York, with the release of *Saved from the Titanic*, a silent film starring *Titanic* survivor Dorothy Gibson. The author writes that since then, the ship's voyage and demise have been used to deliver messages about class, pride and greed, capitalism, the basic conflict between humans and nature, and the inevitability of fate, as well as serving as an all-purpose symbol of doom. Robert Fulford is an arts and op-ed columnist for the *National Post* in Toronto. His books include *Best Seat in the House: Memoirs of a Lucky Man* and *The Triumph of Narrative*.

SOURCE. Robert Fulford, "How *Titanic* Survivor Dorothy Gibson Started a Legacy with Early Film," *National Post*, April 10, 2012.

The blossoming of the *Titanic* into a durable legend of modern times began with the first film, a one-reel silent called *Saved from the Titanic*. A century ago this week, when the great ship collided with an iceberg, one passenger returning from a holiday in Europe was Dorothy Gibson, a 22-year-old actress, singer and artist's model who had made several films. She got into the first lifeboat that left the ship and when she arrived in New York, greeted by squads of newspaper reporters, she knew just what she had to do: Make a movie.

Many more movies have followed, including the successful *A Night to Remember* in 1958 and the much more successful *Titanic*, by James Cameron in 1997, now revived in a 3D version to mark the centennial.

There have also been more than a few TV dramatizations, many poems and songs, an unending stream of magazine articles teasing out the true details of the sinking, and uncountable books on every aspect of the *Titanic*. This year alone there are two biographies of the violinist who led the ship's orchestra, which (the books tell us) either did or did not play the hymn *Nearer My God to Thee* as the ship sank.

Storytellers have discovered that [*Titanic*] carries the weight of any message we care to place upon it.

Over a century the *Titanic* has dug itself more deeply into human consciousness than any other single man-made disaster. It was a major tragedy (some 1,500 people were lost, about 700 survived) but its importance in our collective imagination depends on even more than that. The *Titanic* lives in our memories as a great all-purpose metaphor generator. Storytellers have discovered that it carries the weight of any message we care to place upon it.

Different Meanings from the Same Story

Does it tell us about the class system? On half a dozen occasions I've watched film or TV images of ship's officers

SHOWMAN'S GUIDE
TITANIC
The Rank Organisation presents with pride
Kenneth More in A NIGHT TO REMEMBER

giving preference to first class passengers while steerage passengers try to fight their way out of the lower decks. Does it tell us about the overweening pride of engineers and ship owners? We have all been taught that those poor fools didn't dream such a powerful ship could be sunk by an iceberg and therefore didn't carry nearly enough lifeboats for passengers and crew.

Those who want to see the sinking as a divine judgment on pride and greed can find the appropriate symbols in the details of life on the *Titanic*. Those who look for evidence of upper-class chivalry can enjoy stories of [millionaire businessmen] John Jacob Astor and Benjamin Guggenheim obeying the "women and children first" rule. Those who consider the upper classes decadent and immoral can also find support for their contrary opinions.

The fact that [banker] J. Pierpont Morgan financed and helped plan the *Titanic* provides a reason for saying the story proves the malign power of capitalism. E.J. Pratt, the most renowned Canadian poet of his day, saw it roughly that way in his 1935 poem, *The Titanic*, blaming the "Grey-templed Caesars of the World's Exchange."

Thomas Hardy [an English novelist and poet] chose the man-vs.-nature theme, a popular favourite for many years, in his "Lines on the Loss of the Titanic" [in a poem titled *The Convergence of the Twain*]. He wrote that as "the smart ship grew" the Immanent Will (the blind force driving the universe) prepared its "sinister mate." The meeting of the two sent the ship to the bottom while the iceberg floated on.

Over the years the *Titanic* has been a storyteller's favourite way of signalling doom. In the 1933 Oscar-winning film of Noël Coward's play, *Cavalcade*, about Britain from 1899 to the '30s, a young couple talk lovingly about their future as they lean over a life preserver on a ship's railing. The scene ends with a chilling moment

Image on opposite page: A magazine cover promotes the 1958 film *A Night to Remember*, one of the more successful film adaptations of the *Titanic* disaster. The first such film was released just weeks after the ship sank. (© **Culture Club/ Getty Images**)

A Media Frenzy Greeted the *Titanic*'s Survivors in New York

By the time the *Carpathia* arrived in the New York harbor on April 18 [1912] around 9:15 PM, thousands of people were standing outside Pier 54 at West 13th Street on the Hudson River.

Many were family members of passengers who didn't know if their relatives were dead or alive. Reporters waded in and worked the crowd, interviewing relatives while waiting to catch survivors coming off the ship and record their memories while they were still visceral.

Meanwhile, out in the harbor, more than 50 tugboats jammed with journalists met the *Carpathia* in lower New York harbor. Reporters with megaphones yelled up at the ship, offering $50 or $100 for eyewitness accounts. Photographers' cameras lit up the side of the ship with flashes of magnesium powder.

This was before the rise of radio and movie reels, when newspapers ruled. It was also a Darwinian moment in the history of American journalism.

SOURCE. *Jim O'Grady, "100 Years Ago, Arrival of* Titanic *Survivors in NYC Set Off Media Free-for-All," WNYC, April 15, 2012. www.wnyc.org.*

as they turn away from the railing and the audience reads the ominous label on the life preserver: RMS Titanic.

Dorothy Gibson's Legacy

In 1912 Dorothy Gibson can have had no idea she was starting a grand narrative tradition with *Saved from the Titanic*. When she was finally deposited safely in New York, having been plucked from the lifeboat by the *Carpathia*, she set to work on her movie. It was quickly thrown together at the Éclair studio in Fort Lee, N.J., then the centre of the American movie industry, with Dorothy as both star and scriptwriter and with her lover, Jules Brulatour, as financial backer. Gibson wore on-screen the same white silk evening dress she was wearing when the iceberg interrupted her bridge game.

Released just 29 days after the disaster, *Saved from the Titanic* played to good reviews and audiences in Europe as well as America. Sadly, it's one of the many lost films of the silent era: the only known print was destroyed in a fire at Éclair in 1914.

Gibson gave up movies a few years later and was mostly forgotten when she died in 1946. But in 2005, a biography, *Finding Dorothy*, by Randy Bryan Bigham, revived her reputation. Now [April 2012] she turns up once more as a character in the four-part miniseries made in Budapest as a U.K.-Canada co-production, *Titanic*, now running on Global [a British TV network]. In this version, scripted by Julian Fellowes, Gibson falls in love with the ship's second officer, reassuring him that (unlike many of her fellow passengers) she doesn't worry about class distinctions. She's played by Sophie Winkleman, who shares Gibson's big, heavy-lidded eyes and full lips.

> *Titanic* will still be sailing in its own separate universe, still delivering the metaphors we cherish.

The content Fellowes pours into the script will be familiar to most people who know the *Titanic* story. But Fellowes brings it to fresh life with a clever narrative structure: He has the collision happen four times, so that in each episode we watch a different sampling of characters who all have one thing in common: They are heading for disaster and don't know it.

Two charming young people are falling in love. An anarchist, escaping from the London police, commits murder when someone recognizes him. We learn the secret shame of a highly respectable duke—he's fathered an illegitimate child, though it turns out that his wife has known the truth all along.

When the collision comes they all follow tradition and reveal their true personalities, often improved versions: The countess, previously an *Olympic*-class harridan, reveals herself as essentially decent. So, as the centennial of the sinking arrives this Sunday, the *Titanic* will still be sailing in its own separate universe, still delivering the metaphors we cherish—and Dorothy Gibson will still be on board, heading toward stardom.

VIEWPOINT **10**

Survivors' Own Stories Define *Titanic*'s Legacy

Wade Sisson

The stories of *Titanic* survivors and the lessons that can be learned from their experiences are the true legacy of the disaster. So argues the author of the following viewpoint. He writes that some survivors' stories illustrate heroic and selfless sacrifice, even while others show unfortunate cowardice. Although all survivors had passed away as of the writing of the viewpoint, the author writes that their stories will continue to resonate. As survivor Jack Thayer poetically explained, with *Titanic* the world was roused out of an old era and way of thinking, and the fast-paced though contentious modern era began. Wade Sisson is the author of *Racing Through the Night*, the story of *Olympic* rushing to aid *Titanic*, her sister ship.

They are all gone now—the *Titanic* survivors. No human being who stood on her decks that night remains to commemorate the event on its 100th

---

SOURCE. Wade Sisson, "*Titanic* Survivors: Their Enduring Stories," *Denver Post*, April 16, 2012.

anniversary. Their stories are with us, however, and the lessons remain.

From the moment the world learned the *Titanic* had sunk, we wanted to know: Who had survived? Those answers didn't come until the evening of Thursday, April 18, 1912—when the Cunard liner *Carpathia* finally reached New York with the 705 survivors who had been recovered from *Titanic*'s lifeboats.

Each survivor who descended the gangway had a story to tell—and the world wanted to hear them all. The *New York Times* sent an army of reporters to fill that need—and gave us stories such as that from Harold Bride, "*Titanic*'s surviving wireless man." The junior operator relayed the story of the ship's band. "The way the band kept playing was a noble thing. I heard it first while still we were working wireless when there was a ragtime tune for us, and the last I saw of the band, when I was floating out in the sea with my lifebelt on, it was still on deck playing 'Autumn.' How they ever did it I cannot imagine."

> 'I shall hold her memory dear as my preserver, who preferred to die so that I might live.'

Diverse and Compelling Stories

There were stories of heroism—such as that of Edith Evans, 36, who was waiting to board Collapsible D, the last boat to leave *Titanic*, when she turned to Caroline Brown and said, "You go first. You have children waiting at home." The sacrifice cost Evans her life, but as Mrs. Brown said later, "It was a heroic sacrifice, and as long as I live I shall hold her memory dear as my preserver, who preferred to die so that I might live."

There was cowardice. Most men who survived found themselves trying to explain how they survived when women and children had died, but most of this vitriol was directed at White Star Chairman J. Bruce Ismay, who

Titanic's First-Class Passengers' Code of Honor

In the movie [*Titanic*] as the ship is sinking, the first-class passengers scramble to climb into the small number of lifeboats. Only the determination of the hardy seamen, who use guns to keep the grasping plutocrats at bay, gets the women and children into the boats. In fact, according to survivors' accounts, the "women and children first" convention was observed. . . . Some of the most powerful men in the world adhered to an unwritten code of honor—even though it meant certain death.

The movie-makers altered the story for good reason: No one would believe it today.

SOURCE. *Fareed Zakaria, "When the Upper Class Had Class,"* Across the Board, *November–December 2003, p. 7.*

survived the sinking of the ship he had commissioned. Ostracized by society and haunted by negative press, Ismay remained a virtual recluse for the rest of his life and died at age 74 in 1937.

There was mystery. Two little French boys had been placed aboard Collapsible D by their father, known to those on board as "Mr. Hoffman." Having lost their father, and not being able to speak English or explain who they were, the boys became known as "The *Titanic* Waifs" in photographs that were carried in newspapers worldwide. Their mother back in France recognized her sons and sailed to New York to reclaim them. The boys' father, whose real name was Michel Navratil, had been in the midst of a bitter divorce and had abducted the boys before boarding *Titanic*.

Mostly, there was loss. On her return to New York after picking up *Titanic*'s survivors, *Carpathia* had become known as a ship of widows. Rene Harris, who lost her husband, Broadway producer Henry Harris, in the disaster, later spoke of her loss when she said, "It was not a night to remember. It was a night to forget." Some survivors wrote books so that the world would never forget *Titanic* or her last night.

Published First-Person Accounts

The first books came from Archibald Gracie, who died before *The Truth About the Titanic* was published, and second class passenger Lawrence Beesley, who in *The Loss of the Titanic* wrote that "No living person should seek to dwell in thought for one moment on such a disaster except in the endeavour to glean from it knowledge that will be of profit to the whole world in the future. When such knowledge is practically applied in the construction, equipment and navigation of passenger steamers—and not until then—will be the time to cease to think of the *Titanic* disaster and of the hundreds of men and women so needlessly sacrificed."

> Each life saved contains a lesson for the world.

Others kept in touch through letters or meetings. Gladys Cherry, who along with her cousin the Countess of Rothes left *Titanic* in lifeboat 8, later wrote to Able Seaman Thomas Jones that "The dreadful regret I shall always have, and I know you share with me, is that we ought to have gone back to see whom we could pick up; but if you remember, there was only an American lady, my cousin, self and you who wanted to return."

The *Titanic* haunted her surviving officers, none of whom ever received their own commands, perhaps a consequence of their association with the most famous of shipwrecks.

The wreck was something most *Titanic* survivors preferred not to talk about even to relatives. Most of those who were children in 1912 only began to speak of the disaster late in life. Those who did speak became star guests at events sponsored by the Titanic Historical Society.

The Last Survivor

Millvina Dean was only nine weeks old when she sailed on *Titanic* with her parents and brother. Her father died in the disaster, and the family returned to England, where she lived the rest of her life. "Nobody knew about me and the *Titanic*, to be honest, nobody took any interest, so I took no interest either," Dean said. "But then they found the wreck, and after they found the wreck, they found me." For the last two decades of her life, Dean attended *Titanic* conventions and granted interviews in which she talked about the tragedy that had claimed her father so many years before. She refused to see James Cameron's *Titanic* for fear of memories it would stir about her father. "It would have made me think, did he jump overboard or did he go down with the ship?" she said. "I would have been very emotional."

Millvina had been a star from the moment she was brought aboard *Carpathia*, where women clamored to hold "this lovable mite of humanity," and when she died at age 97 on May 31, 2009, the 98th anniversary of the *Titanic*'s launch, we lost our last living link to the *Titanic*.

They have gone—and we must commemorate the disaster without them, but each life saved contains a lesson for the world.

As survivor Jack Thayer said, "There was peace, and the world had an even tenor to its way. Nothing was revealed in the morning the trend of which was not known the night before. It seems to me that the disaster about to occur was the event that not only made the world rub its eyes and awake but woke it with a start, keeping it moving at a rapidly accelerating pace ever since with less and less peace, satisfaction and happiness. To my mind the world of today awoke April 15th, 1912."

CHAPTER 3

Personal Narratives

VIEWPOINT 1

A Teen First-Class Passenger Writes About the Night *Titanic* Sank

John B. Thayer

The following personal narrative was originally published privately in 1940 for the survivor's family members only. The author was a seventeen-year-old first-class passenger aboard *Titanic* enjoying a pleasant trip in beautiful weather. He writes that on the night of the accident, he went on deck "to see the fun" and was not worried that there were any serious problems on the "unsinkable" ship. He describes witnessing the orderly beginning of the passenger evacuation, which turns much more chaotic later, as passengers become increasingly desperate. He details searching for his family, making sure that his mother gets on a lifeboat, jumping into the freezing water to swim to a lifeboat, and hearing the terrible cries of passengers in life preservers floating in the ocean after *Titanic* sinks. The son of a wealthy railroad executive, John B. Thayer was a banker and also served as financial vice president and treasurer of the University of Pennsylvania.

Photo on previous page: Passengers stroll on the second-class promenade on the deck of *Titanic* in 1912. (© **Popperfoto/ Getty Images.**)

SOURCE. John B. Thayer, *The Sinking of the S.S.* Titanic. Chicago: Academy Chicago Publishers, 1998, pp. 331–356. Reproduced by permission.

My Father, John B. Thayer, Second Vice-President of the Pennsylvania Railroad, my Mother, Marian Longstreth Morris Thayer, my Mother's maid Margaret Fleming, and I, went all in one party that sailed first-class from Southampton. . . . We left Queenstown at one-thirty in the afternoon of Thursday, April 11th. The weather was fair and clear, the ship palatial, the food delicious. Almost everyone was counting the days till we would see the Statue of Liberty.

> It was the kind of a night that made one feel glad to be alive.

I occupied a stateroom adjoining that of my Father and Mother on the port side of "C" deck; and, needless to say, being seventeen years old, I was all over the ship. . . . It had become very much colder [after dinner]. It was a brilliant, starry night. There was no moon and I have never seen the stars shine brighter; they appeared to stand right out of the sky, sparkling like cut diamonds. A very light haze, hardly noticeable, hung low over the water. I have spent much time on the ocean, yet I have never seen the sea smoother than it was that night; it was like a mill-pond, and just as innocent looking, as the great ship quietly rippled through it. I went onto the boat deck—it was deserted and lonely. The wind whistled through the stays, and blackish smoke poured out of the three forward funnels; the fourth funnel was a dummy for ventilation purposes. It was the kind of a night that made one feel glad to be alive. . . .

A Slight Shock and Sudden Quiet

I wound my watch—it was 11:45 PM—and was just about to step into bed, when I seemed to sway slightly. I immediately realized that the ship had veered to port as though she had been gently pushed. If I had had a brimful glass of water in my hand not a drop would have been spilled, the shock was so slight.

Almost instantaneously the engines stopped. The sudden quiet was startling and disturbing. Like the subdued quiet in a sleeping car, at a stop, after a continuous run. Not a sound except the breeze whistling through the half open port. Then there was the distant noise of running feet and muffled voices, as several people hurried through the passageway. Very shortly the engines started up again—slowly—not with the bright vibration to which we were accustomed, but as though they were tired. After very few revolutions they again stopped.

I hurried into my heavy overcoat and drew on my slippers. All excited, but not thinking anything serious had occurred, I called in to my Father and Mother that "I was going up on deck to see the fun." Father said he would put on his clothes and come right up and join me. It was bitterly cold. I walked around the deck looking over the side from time to time. As far as I could see, there was nothing to be seen, except something scattered on the well deck forward, which I afterwards learned was ice. There was no sign of any large iceberg. Only two or three people were on deck when I arrived, but many rapidly gathered. My Father joined me very soon. He and I moved around the deck trying to discover what happened and finally found one of the crew who told us we had hit an iceberg, which he tried to point out to us, but which we could not see in spite of the brilliant night, as possibly our eyes were not accustomed to the dark after coming out of the lighted ship.

> "The band was playing lively tunes without apparently receiving much attention from the worried [passengers]."

The ship took on a very slight list to starboard. We did not know it at the moment, but we learned afterward that the iceberg had ripped open probably four of her larger forward compartments on the starboard side; and also that if we had only hit the ice head on, instead of

Titanic survivors crowd a collapsible lifeboat just before being picked up by the *Carpathia*. (© Universal History Archive/UIG via Getty Images.)

making too late an attempt to avoid it, the ship would in all probability have survived the collision.

About fifteen minutes after the collision she developed a list to port and was distinctly down by the head.

Here we were eight hundred miles out from New York, off the Grand Banks, our position Latitude 41 degrees 46 minutes North, Longitude 50 degrees 14 minutes West. No one yet thought of any serious trouble. The ship was unsinkable. . . .

Evacuation Begins on Deck A

We then hurried up to the lounge on "A" deck, which was not crowded with people, some standing, some hurrying, some pushing out onto deck. My friend Milton Long came by at that time and asked if he could stay with us. There was a great deal of noise. The band was playing lively tunes without apparently receiving much attention from the worried moving audience. . . .

Finally we thought we had better inquire whether or not Mother had been able to get a boat. We went into the hall and happened to meet the Chief Dining-Room Steward. He told us that he had just seen my Mother, and that she had not yet been put into a boat. We found her, and were told that they were loading the forward boats on the port side from the deck below. The ship had a substantial list to port, which made quite a space between the side of the ship and the life boats, swinging out over the water, so the crew stretched folded streamer chairs across the space, over which the people were helped into the boats.

We proceeded to the deck below. Father, Mother, and the maid, went ahead of Long and myself. The lounge on "B" deck was filled with a milling crowd, and as we went through the doorway out onto the deck, people pushed between my Father and Mother, and Long and me. Long and I could not catch up, and were entirely separated from them. I never saw my Father again. . . .

Increasing Chaos as the Ship Sinks

It must now have been about 1:25 AM. The ship was way down by the head with water entirely covering her bow. She gradually came out of her list to port, and if anything, had a slight list to starboard. The crew had commenced to load and lower the forward starboard boats. These could hold over sixty people, but the officers were afraid to load them to capacity, while suspended by falls, bow and stern, sixty feet over the water. They might have buckled, or broken from the falls.

The stern lifeboats, four on the port and four on the starboard side, had already left the ship. One of the first boats to leave carried only twelve people, Sir Cosmo [Edmund Duff Gordon] and Lady Duff Gordon, and ten others. Most of the boats were loaded with about forty to forty-five, with the exception of the last few to go, which were loaded to full capacity.

One could see the boats that had already left the ship, standing off about five or six hundred yards. Apparently there was only one light, about which most of them congregated. They were plainly visible and looked very safe on that calm sea.

On deck, the exhaust steam was still roaring. The lights were still strong. The band, with life preservers on, was still playing. The crowd was fairly orderly. Our own situation was too pressing, the scene too kaleidoscopic for me to retain any detailed picture of individual behavior. I did see one man come through the door out onto the deck with a full bottle of Gordon Gin. He put it to his mouth and practically drained it. If ever I get out of this alive, I thought, there is one man I will never see again. He apparently fought his way into one of the last two boats, for he was one of the first men I recognized upon reaching the deck of the S.S. "CARPATHIA." Someone told me afterward that he was a State Senator or Congressman from Virginia or West Virginia.

> "It was really every man for himself."

There was some disturbance in loading the last two forward starboard boats. A large crowd of men was pressing to get into them. No women were around as far as I could see. I saw [White Star Line chairman J. Bruce] Ismay, who had been assisting in the loading of the last boat, push his way into it. It was really every man for himself. Many of the crew and men from the stokehole were lined up, with apparently not a thought of attempting to get into a boat without orders. Purser H. W. McElroy, as brave and as fine a man as ever lived, was standing up in the next to last boat, loading it. Two men, I think they were dining-room stewards, dropped into the boat from the deck above. As they jumped he fired twice into the air. I do not believe they were hit, but they were quickly thrown out. McElroy did not take a boat and was not saved. I should say that all this took place on "A" deck, just under the boat deck. . . .

Jumping Off Just in Time

It was now about 2:15 AM we could see the water creeping up the deck, as the ship was going down by the head at a pretty fast rate. The water was right up to the bridge. There must have been over sixty feet of it on top of the bow. As the water gained headway along the deck, the crowd gradually moved with it, always pushing, toward the floating stern and keeping in from the rail of the ship as far as they could. We were a mass of hopeless, dazed humanity, attempting, as the Almighty and Nature made us, to keep our final breath until the last possible moment. . . . We had no time to think now, only to act. [Long and I] shook hands, wished each other luck. I said "Go ahead, I'll be right with you." I threw my overcoat off as he climbed over the rail, sliding down facing the ship. Ten seconds later I sat on the rail. I faced out, and with a push of my arms and hands, jumped into the water as far out from the ship as I could. When we jumped we were only twelve or fifteen feet above the water. I never saw Long again. His body was later recovered. I am afraid that the few seconds elapsing between our going, meant the difference between being sucked into the deck below, as I believe he was, or pushed out by the back wash. I was pushed out and then sucked down.

> We were a mass of hopeless, dazed humanity, attempting . . . to keep our final breath until the last possible moment.

The cold was terrific. The shock of the water took the breath out of my lungs. Down and down I went, spinning in all directions.

Swimming as hard as I could in the direction which I thought to be away from the ship, I finally came up with my lungs bursting, but not having taken any water. The ship was in front of me, forty yards away. How long I had been swimming under water, I don't know. Perhaps a minute or less. Incidentally, my watched stopped at 2:22 AM.

Praise for the Disciplined Crew

The story would not be complete without comment on the discipline and behavior of the crew. They were perfect and did their full and complete duty. To see all the men covered with the dirt and grime of the boiler room, after having drawn the fires from the flooded stokehole, lined up on deck, awaiting orders, was a grand, inspiring sight. It was a tribute to the British Mercantile Marine.

Not a single Engineering Officer or Engineer of the ship was saved. Everyone was at his post in the engine room. They kept the lights going till the ship went under. They made the power for the "C.Q.D.," which called for help through the night. Think what panic we might have had if the lights had failed; or worse yet, if the S.S. "CARPATHIA" had been unable to hear our call and learn our position. . . .

Titanic Vanishes into the Sea

Her deck was turned slightly toward us [the overturned lifeboat Thayer grabbed on to]. We could see groups of the almost fifteen hundred people still aboard, clinging in clusters or bunches, like swarming bees; only to fall in masses, pairs or singly, as the great after part of the ship, two hundred and fifty feet of it, rose into the sky, till it reached a sixty-five or seventy degree angle. Here it seemed to pause, and just hung, for what felt like minutes. Gradually she turned her deck away from us, as though to hide from our sight the awful spectacle.

We had an oar on our overturned boat. In spite of several men working it, amid our cries and prayers, we were being gradually sucked in toward the great pivoting mass. I looked upwards—we were right underneath the three enormous propellers. For an instant, I thought they were sure to come right down on top of us. Then with the deadened noise of the bursting of her last gallant bulkheads, she slid quietly away from us into the sea.

There was no final apparent suction, and practically no wreckage that we could see.

> [The] terrible continuing cry lasted for twenty or thirty minutes, gradually dying away.

I don't remember all the wild talk and calls that were going on on our boat, but there was one concerted sigh or sob as she went from view.

Probably a minute passed with almost dead silence and quiet. Then an individual call for help, from here, from there; gradually swelling into a composite volume of one long continuous wailing chant, from the fifteen hundred in the water all around us. It sounded like locusts on a mid-summer night, in the woods in Pennsylvania. . . .

The Hundreds Dead Who Did Not Drown

This terrible continuing cry lasted for twenty or thirty minutes, gradually dying away, as one after another could no longer withstand the cold and exposure. Practically no one was drowned, as no water was found in the lungs of those later recovered. Everyone had on a life preserver.

The partially filled lifeboats standing by, only a few hundred yards away never came back. Why on earth they did not come back is a mystery. How could any human being fail to heed those cries? They were afraid the boats would be swamped by people in the water.

The most heartrending part of the whole tragedy was the failure, right after the "TITANIC" sank, of those boats which were only partially loaded, to pick up the poor souls in the water. There they were, only four or five hundred yards away, listening to the cries, and still they did not come back. If they had turned back several hundred more would have been saved. No one can explain it. It was not satisfactorily explained in any investigation. It was just one of the many "Acts of God" running through the whole disaster.

During this time more and more were trying to get aboard the bottom of our overturned boat. We helped them on until we were packed like sardines. Then out of self-preservation, we had to turn some away. There were finally twenty-eight of us altogether on board. We were very low in the water. The water had roughened up slightly, and was occasionally washing over us. The stars still shone brilliantly.

A *Titanic* Stewardess Describes the Evacuation

Violet Jessup

The only person known to have survived two major ocean liner disasters—*Titanic*'s sinking in 1912 and the *Britannic* explosion in 1916—authored this viewpoint. In the following excerpt from her memoir, she discusses working on *Titanic* the night of the collision with the iceberg. Shortly after the accident, she is roused from her quarters and back to work. She describes helping the passengers in her section with their lifebelts while reassuring them that it is just a precaution. She also recounts her experience on deck, where passengers initially seem reluctant to board lifeboats and be lowered from the ship. The evacuation gains speed and urgency, as it becomes clear that the ship really is sinking. An experienced stewardess for the White Star Line, Violet Jessup worked as a stewardess on all three of its Olympic-class ocean liners.

SOURCE. Violet Jessup, Titanic *Survivor: The Newly Discovered Memoirs of Violet Jessup Who Survived Both the* Titanic *and* Britannic *Disasters*. Dobbs Ferry, NY: Sheridan House, 1997.

It was all so happy and peaceful. If the sun did fail to shine so brightly on the fourth day out, and if a little cold nip crept into the air as evening set in, it only served to emphasize the warmth and luxuriousness within. On that Sunday evening, the music was at its gayest, led by young Jock the first violin; when I ran into him during the interval, he laughingly called out to me in his rich Scotch accent, that he was about to give them a "real tune, a Scotch tune, to finish up with." Always so eager and full of life was Jock.

Grayish skies replaced sunshine but the calm sea continued, a calmness that only the ocean knows: Perfect serenity for miles, broken by the rhythm of the water lazily lapping against the ship's side, as her great hulk clove through it.

Colder and yet a little colder, gray sky deepening into haziness as evening fell, making the water look like molten silver as it caught the soft beams of a misty moon.

A soothing peace and an ever increasing chill set in that drove one indoors, an excuse for bed and a good book.

I slipped out on deck, my nightly custom before retiring, for a few moments alone with my thoughts. It was all so quiet, but how penetratingly cold it had become! Little wisps of mist like tiny fairies wafted gently inboard from the sea and left my face clammy. I shivered. It was indeed a night for bed, warmth and cozy thoughts of home and firesides. I thought of the man in the crow's nest as I came indoors, surely an unenviable job on such a night. . . .

Called to Duty After the Crash

At the end, my book closed, I lay lazily reflecting on many things, comfortably drowsy.

Crash! . . . Then a low, rending, crunching, ripping sound as *Titanic* shivered a trifle and the sound of her engines gently ceased.

Quiet, dead silence for a minute. Then doors opened and voices could be heard in gentle enquiry. Quietly, restrained voices passed our door, answered just as quietly. . . .

Suddenly, there was movement. Men were returning to duty they had but recently left. I realized that I too, must hasten on duty, for I had quite a number of women in my section.

Ann [Thurnbull, her cabinmate] and I started to dress rapidly and in silence. My teeth chattered a little and I found my fingers were all thumbs.

Good, faithful old Stanley, one of my bedroom stewards, came knocking at the door, his face whiter than usual as he remarked casually, "I'm calling all our people, sister." He always addressed me as sister when we were alone. "Anything you'd like me to do for you on my way? You know the ship is sinking?"

"Sinking? Of course *Titanic* couldn't be sinking! What nonsense!"

Sinking? The word repeated itself without fully entering my understanding as I finished putting on my uniform and quickly followed Stanley to our section.

Sinking? Of course *Titanic* couldn't be sinking! What nonsense! She so perfect, so new—yet now she was so still, so inanimate; not a sound after that awful grinding crash. She that had so short a time ago been so vital was not the embodiment of immobility.

My mind, usually adjustable to sudden and unforeseen happenings, could not accept the fact that this superperfect creation was to do so futile a thing as sink. Automatically, I untied and readjusted a child's lifebelt, much to the little one's interest and sleepy bewilderment.

Helping the Passengers

I continued through my section trying to reassure, answering questions to which there seemed no answer.

Everywhere I found extraordinary calmness. To satisfy my pride, I assumed an indifference to facts all too obvious. People who had been asleep were dressing, fumbling sleepy-eyed with buttons. They were unemotional, probably thinking as I did that it was all too fantastic. Those who had not yet retired for the night were standing in groups on the companion square, chatting in the restrained, well-bred manner of the day.

Suddenly orders came down, striking a deeper chill to the consciousness. Everybody to the boats, but just as a precautionary measure, of course.

We continued to fix lifebelts, reminding people to put on warm clothing, take blankets and valuables. Yes, of course, we reiterated from room to room, just a precautionary measure!

Yes, of course, we reiterated from room to room, just a precautionary measure!

Reluctantly, slowly, people started up the companions, still inclined to chat by the way, some joking and quite unhurried, taking their time about it. From above, officers' anxious faces peered down, loathe to give undue alarm but wishing people would bestir themselves. To those few who showed concern, a reassuring answer was forthcoming: "There are plenty of boats in the vicinity; they'll be with us any moment now." Those dear youngsters in the cabin opposite ours thought it all was a "grand show."

All passengers upstairs at last, I looked around. There was no sound, *Titanic* as steady as a rock; she might have been in dock and all the crew gone home. I returned to my room and found Ann.

What to do next? Absently, I began tidying up, folding my nightgown, putting things in their place, when I saw Stanley at the door again, watching me. Then he almost shouted as he seized my arm: "My God, don't you realize that this ship will sink, that she has struck an iceberg, that you have to follow the rest upstairs as quickly as possible?" . . .

Waiting to Board the Lifeboats

Out on deck, the first arguments started over who would and who wouldn't go into the boats which appeared to be suspended miles above the yawning blackness below.

Nobody was anxious to move; *Titanic* seemed so steady. To justify their reluctance, some pointed to a light on the horizon: another ship's lights! People were reassured, content to bide their time.

One boat was already being lowered with very few people in it. When this was pointed out as a shining example for backward souls by the officer near me, he got a rather alarming response as the crowd surged forward to embark. The boat was lowered very full, almost too full this time; and so on. Always, some held back in need of coaxing while a few were too eager.

A steward stood waiting with his back to the bulkhead, cigarette in mouth and hands in his pockets. It struck me forcibly as the first time I had ever seen a steward stand thus amid a group of distinguished guests.

A woman standing near me gave an approving glance as [multimillionaire businessman] John Jacob Astor handed his wife into a boat, waving encouragingly to her as he stepped back into an ever-increasing crowd of men.

Ann Turnbull, still silent and unmoved, dragged a little behind me. I suggested we keep together and we stood awhile to watch. There was nothing else we could do. Dimly I heard a shot.

Glancing forward I caught my breath as a white rocket shot up, then another. Distress rockets! They went very high with great noise. The lights on the horizon seemed to come nearer. That cheered up the group about us, who had slowly started to fill a boat. Young officers urged them to greater speed, showing unlimited patience, I thought. Another rocket went up into the night.

A few women near me started to cry loudly when they realized a parting had to take place, their husbands standing silently by. They were Poles and could not understand a word of English. Surely a terrible plight, to be among a crowd in such a situation and not be able to understand anything that is being said.

> I noticed the forward part of [*Titanic*] was lower now, much lower!

Boats were now being lowered more rapidly and a crowd of foreigners was brought up by a steward from the third class. They dashed eagerly as one man over to a boat, almost more than the officer could control. But he regained order and managed to get the boat away. It descended slowly, uncertainly at first, now one end up and then the other; the falls were new and difficult to handle. Some men nearby were throwing things over the side—deck chairs, rafts or any wooden thing lying nearby.

Suddenly, the crowd of people beside me parted. A man dashed to the ship's side, and before anyone could stop him, hurled himself into the descending boat. There was a murmur of amazement and disapproval.

Realizing That *Titanic* Truly Is Sinking

I turned to say something to Ann. Looking along the length of the ship, I noticed the forward part of her was lower now, much lower! For a fraction of a second, my heart stood still, as is often the case when faith, hitherto unshaken faith, gets its first setback.

One of the mailmen from our sorting office joined us. His work was finished, he remarked unemotionally. "The mail is floating up to F-deck with the water," he told us.

I tried not to hear what he said, not wanting to believe what he accepted so stoically. Instead, I listened to the faint sounds of music from Jock's men. They were playing Nearer My God to Thee.

Boarding a Lifeboat

My arm was suddenly jerked and I turned to see young Mason who had been busy filling a boat. His face looked weary and tired, but he gave a bright smile as he ordered my group into the boat, calling out "Good luck!" as we stepped in, helped by his willing, guiding hand. I nearly fell over the tackle and oars as I tried to assist Ann in beside me. She was suffering with her feet, I could see, and found her lifebelt got in the way of moving freely.

'Look after this, will you?' and I reached out to receive somebody's forgotten baby in my arms.

Before I could do anything, young Mason hailed me and held up something, calling as he prepared to throw it, "Look after this, will you?" and I reached out to receive somebody's forgotten baby in my arms.

It started to whimper as I pressed it to me, the hard cork surface of the lifebelt being anything but a comfort, poor mite. The boat was full now, full of people with dull, inquiring faces. I spoke to one woman but she shook her head, not understanding a word I said.

Groaning, the boat descended a fearful distance into that inky blackness beneath, intensified as the lights fell on it occasionally.

"Surely it is all a dream," I thought as I looked up the side of the ship, beautifully illuminated, each deck alive with lights; the dynamos were on the top deck. I tried to make myself believe it could not be true, all this. I even noticed a few people leaning over the rail, watching in an unconcerned manner; perhaps they too were persuading themselves it was a bad dream!

VIEWPOINT 3

Survivors Share *Titanic* Escape Stories

New York Post

The following viewpoint contains excerpts of *Titanic* survivors' accounts as reported in a local newspaper the day after *Carpathia* arrived in New York. Judging from their stories, survivors who were able to leave the ship early were spared the more chaotic experiences of those who left later in the evacuation. Passengers describe the lifeboat boarding process, hearing gunshots, watching the ship sinking, and seeing fellow passengers die of exposure in the cold water. Many of the survivors interviewed express the same sentiment: that no one believed *Titanic* would sink. The *New York Post* is a daily newspaper established in 1801 and one of the oldest newspapers in the country.

Survivors of the *Titanic* gave accounts of the scene on that night of tragedy which varied widely. People in different parts of the great ship seem to

---

SOURCE. "*Titanic*: Stories of the Rescued," *New York Post*, April 19, 1912. Reproduced by permission.

have borne themselves very differently. Further, some of the survivors who left the ship with the earlier boats seem to have missed some terrible and tragic experiences which befell those who were present at the last desperate rush for safety. Thus, according to some, the getting into the boats was almost orderly. It seems agreed that those who first entered the boats did not believe they would be needed—did not realise that the great ship was really going to sink.

However, the doctor of the *Carpathia* tells of picking up one boat full of stokers, except for two women.

> '[*Titanic*'s] lights still burning brightly, the picture, with the iceberg as a background, was most beautiful.'

Both men and women, according to the accounts of several survivors, were piled into the first lifeboats which left the *Titanic* after the crash. This accounts for the large number of men saved. Many who got into the boats early did so in a semi-joking spirit, according to several accounts. There was thought to be no danger whatsoever, and getting out in lifeboats was considered an extra precaution. So men, as well as women, got aboard without the feeling that they were doing anything cowardly.

Watching the Steamer Sink

Here is the account given by Max Frohlicher Stehle, who, with his wife and daughter, was among the survivors.

> We had left the saloon and retired to our stateroom, but none of us had gone to sleep, when we were suddenly thrown to the floor. Putting on the few clothes we could find, we made our way to the deck. The ship was slowly sinking. The lifeboats were being lowered. My wife and two other women entered one of the first boats lowered. Twelve men, including myself, were standing near. As there were no other women passengers waiting to get

into the boats at that time, we were asked to accompany the women.

While we got into the boats for safety, all of us thought we would be able to return to the *Titanic*. The sea was calm. We were rowed by the four members of the crew who were in charge of the lifeboat, about three hundred yards from the *Titanic*.

While we were rowing away from the steamer, her lights still burning brightly, the picture, with the iceberg as a background, was most beautiful. . . . The steamer slowly sank, the bow sinking beneath the surface first. The water was covered with small boats and rafts. The ship sank until the front half was buried beneath the water. There was a loud crash. The lights went out. Other people, who left the boat, later say that she broke in two.

After the boat had sunk, we began to search for food or other provisions. There was nothing edible in the lifeboats. We could not find even fresh water. Fortunately, one of the men had some stimulant with him, which was given to the women. After drifting around for what seemed weeks, the *Carpathia* was sighted coming toward us. We had no matches or lanterns, and it was not until daylight that we were put aboard the rescuing ship. . . .

Panic and Gunshots

This was the story of Edwards Beans of Glasgow:

My wife was in bed when the crash came, and I went on deck. We saw the iceberg as plainly as we can see here on the pier. The *Titanic* was making about eighteen knots an hour when she struck. The berg was thirty or forty feet above the water. Fifteen minutes after the first shock, there was an explosion in the boiler-room and half an hour later two more. The stern of the boat floated about an hour and three-quarters before it went down. I heard a report that two steerage passengers had been shot when they started to crowd women away from the boats.

Washington Dodge of San Francisco, who was saved, with his wife and son, Washington, Jr., four years old, gave this version of the disaster. . . .

Everybody seemed to be panic stricken and there was a rush for the boats. I heard a lot of shots, but I do not know where they came from. In fact, it was not until later on the *Carpathia* that I recalled the shots. When I saw the boat was sinking, I ran back to my cabin, where I had left my wife and child, but, to my horror, they were gone. I saw hundreds of people running about, but I did not see my family. I searched all over for them, but could not find them. I was on deck, and they were getting ready to lower a lifeboat. They called for women to fill three seats left but there were no more women on that deck. Then a man shoved me into the boat, and I gave my wife and son up for lost.

'I did not know my wife and son had been rescued until we met on board the *Carpathia*. I cannot describe our meeting.'

I did not know my wife and son had been rescued until we met on board the *Carpathia*. I cannot describe our meeting.

Nobody thought that the *Titanic* was going to sink. . . . In the lifeboat we hoped for rescue, for all we knew that the wireless had sent out our call for help, and that the call had been answered. In the morning, we saw the *Carpathia* in the distance coming toward us, and a little while later saw her passengers crowding the rail looking for us. . . .

Swimming to a Waterlogged Lifeboat

George Rheins of no. 417 Fifth Avenue, New York, who was on the *Titanic* with his brother-in-law, Joseph Holland Loring of London, said no one seemed to know, for twenty minutes after the boat struck, that anything had happened. Many of the passengers stood round for an hour with their lifebelts on, he said, and saw people getting in the boats. When all the boats had gone, he added, he shook hands with his brother-in-law, who would not jump, and leaped over the side of the boat.

He swam for a quarter of an hour and reached a boat and climbed in. He found the boat, with eighteen occupants, half under water. The people were in water up to their knees. Seven of them, he said, died during the night, only those standing remaining alive. After six hours in the cold water the situation became critical, because the boat was sinking. Four bodies were left in the boat when it was picked up by the *Carpathia* he said.

Everyone Could Have Been Saved

[W.J.] Hawksford, who was a second-cabin passenger, said that when the boat struck the iceberg, it did not do so with a jar, but there was more of a bumping and grinding sensation. He said that there was absolutely no confusion on board, the passengers who were in their staterooms going on the deck, and on being assured that there was no danger the most of them went back to their rooms.

> A short time after, I do not know just how long, we were again called and told to put on the lifebelts, and then we went on deck, and all the women who could be found were placed in the lifeboats. There was not a man attempted to get into one of the boats before the women and the children were in. If there had been enough lifeboats, everyone would have been saved. There was plenty of time.

VIEWPOINT 4

My Grandfather, the *Titanic*'s Violinist

Christopher Ward

The following viewpoint describes the aftermath of the *Titanic* disaster and how it continues to affect the author's family one hundred years later. The author's grandfather, Jock Hume, was a musician who died on *Titanic*, leaving a pregnant fiancée and a family in disarray. Instead of sympathy and support, White Star Line, *Titanic*'s owner, sent the author's great-grandfather a bill for Hume's uniform and offered to ship the body back to the United Kingdom for a fee. The viewpoint illustrates that the author's family's experience was not unique. The author describes a number of episodes of inhumane behavior toward working-class members of crews and steerage passengers of *Titanic* and other ships. Christopher Ward is a former editor of the *Daily Express*, a British daily newspaper. He is the author of *And the Band Played On: The* Titanic *Violinist and the Glovemaker: A True Story of Love, Loss, and Betrayal*, a historical account of the catastrophic impact of the disaster on his family.

SOURCE. Christopher Ward, "My Grandfather, the *Titanic*'s Violinist," *The Spectator*, August 6, 2011.

When he died, the White Star Line sent a bill for his uniform.

There can be few better places to consider the irony of the phrase 'the good old days' than Fairview Lawn Cemetery in Halifax, Nova Scotia, where I went last week to visit the grave of my grandfather, a 21-year-old violinist in the band of the White Star liner *Titanic*. More than 120 passengers and crew are buried here, 40 of them still unidentified as we approach the centenary of *Titanic*'s sinking.

The body of Jock Hume, my grandfather, was one of 190 recovered by the cable ship *Mackay-Bennett* and brought back to Halifax (more than a thousand bodies were never found). The corpses of first-class passengers—including that of the American millionaire Jacob Astor—were unloaded from the ship in coffins and driven to the mortuary in horse-drawn hearses. Those of the crew and of steerage passengers had been thrown on to ice in the hold for the sea journey, and were carried off in handcarts on arrival.

> The aftermath . . . is a story more shocking than the sinking itself.

The day the *Mackay-Bennett* docked, Jock's father in Dumfries received a 5s 4d bill for his son's uniform. Jock's pay was stopped the moment the ship went down at 2.20 AM, and the wages owed to him were insufficient to cover the cost of the brass buttons on his bandsman's tunic. When the family asked if his body could be brought home, they were told that 'normal cargo rates' would apply.

Early last year, with a growing sense of my own mortality, I began compiling a 'Who Do You Think You Are?' ring binder for my children and grandchildren, sketching out a family tree whose branches were bowed with farm-labourers from Dumfries and builders from St Helens. But the project came to an abrupt halt when

Hundreds of bodies recovered from the *Titanic* disaster were brought to Halifax, Nova Scotia. One hundred and fifty of the remains—some of them unidentified, as in the headstone in this photo—are buried there. (© **Andrew Bain/ Lonely Planet Images/ Getty Images.**)

I started looking at the circumstances of my mother's birth, six months after the *Titanic* had foundered. Jock's death had been no ordinary one.

The binder was temporarily abandoned for an 80,000-word book about what happened after the *Titanic* sank. No one, I realised, had written about the aftermath. It is a story more shocking than the sinking itself, the class system operating as ruthlessly in death as it did in life. No letters of regret or sympathy were sent to the families of the dead, no personal visits made to grieving families, no Murdoch-style apologetic advertisements taken by the White Star Line. Almost a century later, in fact, no one has said sorry.

The chairman, Bruce Ismay, who saved his own life by jumping into a lifeboat with women and children, never accepted personal or corporate responsibility, although he had taken the decision to remove 16 lifeboats that would have saved most of those on board. He spent the rest of his life pursuing his passions of fishing and grouse shooting. At the Borders Book Festival earlier in the summer—Ismay, too, is the subject of a new book—a cheer went up when I invited comparisons with the management style of Fred the Shred.

If White Star learned nothing from the consequences of its recklessness, its employees did.

But the *Titanic* revealed changing social attitudes, as well as atavistic ones. Andrew Hume, for instance, did not pay the bill for his son's uniform. He forwarded it to the Amalgamated Musicians Union, which published it without comment in its newsletter. Public opinion was beginning to assert itself. More than 30,000 people lined the streets of Colne in Lancashire for the funeral of the liner's bandmaster, Wallace Hartley, who, with the rest of the band, had heroically played until the end to maintain calm.

If White Star learned nothing from the consequences of its recklessness, its employees did. A week after the sinking, 54 stokers and firemen, most of whom had lost a father, a son or a brother, walked off the White Star liner *Olympic* when they discovered there were insufficient lifeboats to accommodate the passengers and crew. They were arrested for mutiny, but the magistrates discharged them. They returned to the *Olympic*, whose departure had been delayed by a fortnight, to find 16 additional lifeboats.

The captain and crew of the *Mackay-Bennett* also discovered that the old order was changing. Having risked their lives sailing more than a thousand miles into ice fields, they might have expected to return to Halifax as heroes. Instead, they were the subjects of a public storm, for they had come back with only 190 corpses, having buried 116 at sea. What made the difference between a body being tipped overboard and one being brought ashore? The purser's conscientious descriptions provided the explanation: tattoos or a foreign-sounding name.

Despite the famous order 'women and children first', more than a third of the children on the *Titanic* died. Yet every child travelling first class and second class was saved. It is a disconcerting statistic of which the *Halifax Echo*, in the immediate aftermath, was unaware. 'Famous Men Chose Death That Penniless Women Might Be Saved', it reported. 'Men of substance and wealth' had sacrificed their lives 'for the sabot-shod illiterate peasant women of Europe'. In fact the highest casualty rate (140 out of 154) was among men travelling second class—in percentage terms greater even than that of the crew, many of whom were needed to man the lifeboats. Their middle-class sense of honour and decency exceeded that of their first-class fellow passengers.

> 'He remained at his post of duty, seeking to save others regardless of his own life.'

The trouble with turning over ancestral stones that have lain undisturbed for nearly a century is that you discover some uncomfortable truths about your own family, too. Jock, I learned, had been playing on passenger liners since he was 15. He left behind a pregnant fiancée, two feuding families, and an adoring younger sister, Kate, who went mad with grief after his death. In the opening weeks of the first world war, to punish her father and stepmother, Kate faked her sister's murder and mutilation by Germans; she was then arrested under the Defence of the Realm Act, on a charge for which the maximum penalty was death by firing squad.

If you ever visit Halifax, do go to Fairview Lawn Cemetery. Jock's grave is number 193, marked by a modest granite block. He is in good company. A few yards away is his schoolfriend Tom Mullin, also 21: when Tom lost a job in the tweed mills due to failing eyesight, Jock got him on to the *Titanic* as a steward. Either side of Jock are a fireman and an engineer, numbered but still unnamed, who died, like him, doing their duty.

As, indeed, did Ernest Freeman, secretary to Bruce Ismay, also a few yards away. Freeman's headstone, paid for by his employer, is one of the more substantial monuments here. 'He remained at his post of duty, seeking to save others regardless of his own life,' says the inscription. One wonders how Ismay felt, back behind his office desk, as he dictated this tribute to Freeman's replacement.

VIEWPOINT 5

An Artist Visits *Titanic* with a Movie Crew in 2001

Ken Marschall

The author of the following viewpoint recounts part of his experience on a 2001 deep-sea expedition to the wreck of *Titanic*. He explains that the project was conducted primarily to capture footage for James Cameron's IMAX 3D documentary *Ghosts of the Abyss*. He describes the groundbreaking vessels, cameras, and other equipment used during the dives. Over the course of seven weeks, the group captured more than nine hundred hours of video, and the author made three detailed and annotated diagrams of *Titanic*. Contrary to common belief, he writes, the debris fields near the ship's wreck hold many undiscovered treasures. Ken Marschall is a painter, illustrator, and film visual effects artist best known for photorealist renderings of ocean liners. He is coauthor with Robert D. Ballard of *Titanic: An Illustrated History* and has served as a consultant on three *Titanic* documentaries.

SOURCE. Ken Marschall, "James Cameron's *Titanic* Expedition 2001: What We Saw on and Inside the Wreck," Marconigraph.com, 2001.

On September 29, 2001, I returned from a nearly seven-week-long expedition to *Titanic* with James Cameron and his team from Earthship Productions, a long-anticipated follow-up to his first exploration in 1995. As before, he utilized the Russian research vessel *Akademik Mstislav Keldysh* and its two deep submersibles *Mir 1* and *Mir 2*. The goal: to get high-definition digital 3D video of the exterior of the bow and stern sections and debris field, illuminated from above by a maneuverable lighting platform called *Medusa*, and to employ two new, state-of-the-art mini ROVs [remotely operated vehicles] for deep interior exploration far exceeding that of any earlier attempt. In addition, small "lipstick" cameras specially mounted inside each submersible recorded the interior drama, and outside *Mir 2*, a high-quality Osprey video camera would supplement Cameron's 3D photography.

State-of-the-Art Technology

The HD 3D system is brand new and cutting edge, developed by Cameron, Sony, and Panavision, and adapted by Pace Technologies. It is of such high resolution that it can be transferred to large-format 70mm film and actually *look like film*, I am told. The lighting platform *Medusa*, manufactured by Phoenix Engineering, provided a high-altitude diffuse light source designed to illuminate a wider area of the wreck than ever before, bathing it in an eerie "moonlight." Suspended on miles of tether from the vessel M.T. *Eas*, *Medusa* is an ROV itself and has its own controllable color camera capable of zooming in on targets below. The two mini ROVs, engineered by Michael Cameron and his team at Dark Matter and dubbed *Jake* and *Elwood*, are about the size of the proverbial bread box and are bright blue and lime green,

> I can say with confidence that the film will be absolutely jaw dropping, no doubt of it.

respectively. They each have dual-beam offset lights and are capable of high-quality video. They were not designed for still photography. The high-definition and other video will be seen in the 45-minute large-format documentary *Ghosts of the Abyss*, to be released in late 2002. In addition, a 90-minute video and DVD are being considered for home distribution following the film.

Having put on 3D glasses and watched the footage aboard *Keldysh* only hours after it was taken, I can say with confidence that the film will be absolutely jaw dropping, no doubt of it. Cameron himself exclaimed after his first dive this year that he got more good shots in the first *hour* down there than during the *whole month* he was out there in '95! The high-definition video is truly breathtaking. The way Cameron illuminated the wreck. . . . Well, you can imagine. As he says, "Lighting is everything." I'll bet many people won't believe some of the scenes are real. They'll swear they were staged, carefully lighted, special-effects-miniature sequences left over from Digital Domain's work on the movie *Titanic*. The 3D is so dramatic, so evident, even with objects far from the camera. Yet the distance between the two camera lenses is only 2.75 inches, the same as human eyes. The result is an awesome view of *Titanic* exactly as one really would see it—far better, actually, than the limited glimpse one gets from the subs' small viewports.

With all the various cameras combined, some 900 hours of video were shot over the course of the expedition. Ed Marsh, Cameron's capable editor, who has been cutting and archiving the footage from the moment it was retrieved from the cameras, has a very long road ahead of him. . . .

Personal Duties During the Expedition

Twelve tandem dives were planned and carried out with *Mir 1* and *Mir 2*, a total of 24. The ROVs were used on many of these. *Elwood* suffered technical problems after the first dive or two, and it fell to *Jake* to carry out further ROV penetrations, which it did flawlessly. It was generally felt that despite a very aggressive schedule and all those weeks in close quarters, the team got along well. They were a great bunch of very talented people, real team players. Cameron told us at the end that of all the films he has worked on, he felt that this crew was the most dedicated.

> I brought a stack of binders full of archival images and numerous plans. While at sea, I created three 'maps.'

My main jobs on board were wreck and artifact identification, assisting with dive planning and, as it evolved, guiding the pilot of *Mir 2* in lighting the exact spots of the ship, often through portholes, where the ROVs were exploring inside. I brought a stack of binders full of archival images and numerous plans. While at sea, I created three "maps" of the bow section (overhead, port, and starboard), each with a lettered and numbered grid to allow the *Mir*, *Medusa*, and *Keldysh* teams to coordinate with each other. I also made a fourth grid map, this one of the stern.

I participated in one third of the dives; i.e., four of the twelve. On each of them, I was in *Mir 2* and had Evgeny "Genya" Cherniev as pilot. He assisted in the designing and building of the *Mir*s in the late 1980s and is an expert pilot. My fellow submariners on my four dives were Lewis Abernathy, who played the character Lewis Bodine in the movie *Titanic*; Don Lynch; and, on the last two dives, Mike Cameron.

The Effect of the 9/11 Terrorist Attacks

I was down on the bow section with Don on September 11. Upon our recovery around 9 PM we emerged jubilant from a successful dive to rescue one of the ROVs, *Elwood*, from deep inside *Titanic*'s Reception Room. *Jake* had once again performed like a champ. Our joy and triumph were instantly shattered when members of our team rushed forward to tell us of the horrific nightmare that had been visited upon us that day [of the terrorists attacks on] New York and Washington, D.C. There was disbelief, then tears, hugs . . . and rage. No accident or act of nature, this disaster was something deliberately engineered by thinking people—no, *monsters*—many of them, over a long period of time. Calculated, coldly premeditated. I was, and continue to be, so angry I can hardly express it.

After the terrorist attack, the Russian crew were very supportive. The director of the P.P. Shirshov Institute of Oceanology (Russian Academy of Sciences), which operates *Keldysh*, wasted no time faxing us a moving letter of condolence. Sergey Kudriashov, the ship's resident videographer whom I had come to know and like, hugged me and said, "We one people, you and me. Be strong."

> I saw the sole of a woman's shoe, looking almost new. . . . Anything one can imagine—it's all down there.

You can imagine how isolated and lonely we felt out there at that moment. For all we knew, it was the beginning of a third world war. We all ached to be home with loved ones; yet at the same time, we knew we were safest where we were. Many satellite phone calls were made and options considered. We immediately headed back to St. John's, Newfoundland but, in the end, with flights grounded, especially international ones—we'd be flying home from Canada—it was decided to carry on with the mission. I'm glad we did. Four more successful dives followed before we finally left the *Titanic* site on September 24. . . .

Artifact Treasures Abound on the Ocean Floor

I've occasionally heard the cynical comment that most of the "good stuff" has been salvaged from the debris field, that very little is left. Nothing could be farther from the truth. Yes, there have been many, many visits. One comes across quite a number of submarine tracks in the sediment, but most of the debris I saw both this year and last, by far, had never been disturbed. Some of the highlights I observed from *Mir 2* this summer during my few, brief moments over the debris field include a set of undamaged whistles with steam pipe and funnel remains next to it, lying in plain view; a cut-glass carafe; numerous china cups; an almost perfectly intact, glistening porcelain toilet; and many other objects and ship fittings. I saw the sole of a woman's shoe, looking almost new. Others saw more shoes. . . . Anything one can imagine—it's all down there.

Studying ANGUS [Acoustically Navigated Geological Underwater Survey, a deep-water camera sled] images at Woods Hole [Oceanographic Institute in Massachusetts] in 1986, I counted nine sections of the elaborate iron and gilt staircase balustrade scattered in the field, many looking undamaged. In a few cases their gilt-bronze detailing brightly reflected the strobe light above. Yet not one of these, to my knowledge, has been found or photographed up close during a manned expedition, much less recovered. . . . I take it back—*Here* is a nice discovery: Cameron came across the steel cover for hatch No. 1 about 250 feet north of the bow, he says, and in line with it. I had noticed what I thought might be it years ago in the corner of an ANGUS image, looking down on it from way above, but it's great to see it so closely and in 3D. It looks to be in good condition and is upside down, puckered in on one side. The one or two ports I could make out in the high-definition video were unbroken. It's tempting to want to replace it where it belongs—on *Titanic*'s forecastle.

CHRONOLOGY

1907	White Star Line decides to build three Olympic-class ocean liners. The super-sized and ultra-luxury ships are to be called *Olympic*, *Titanic*, and *Britannic*.
1909	Construction begins on *Olympic* and *Titanic* at the Harland and Wolff shipyard in Belfast, Ireland.
May 1911	*Olympic* has its maiden voyage, and the hull of *Titanic* is launched.
March 1912	*Titanic* construction is completed.
April 2, 1912	*Titanic* sea trials begin in Belfast.
April 3, 1912	*Titanic* arrives in Southampton, England.
April 10, 1912	*Titanic* sets sail on its maiden voyage from Southampton. It makes additional stops in Cherbourg, France, and Queenstown (now Cobb), Ireland, on its way to New York City.
April 12–13, 1912	*Titanic* sails in calm waters on the North Atlantic.
April 14, 1912	*Titanic* receives seven iceberg warnings during the day.
April 14–15, 1912	11:40 PM: Lookout Frederick Fleet spots an iceberg straight ahead. *Titanic* strikes the iceberg on the starboard (right) side of the bow.
	12 AM: Captain Edward Smith is told the ship will stay afloat only for a couple more hours. Smith orders a call for help via wireless transmission.

12:05 AM: Captain Smith orders that the lifeboats be uncovered and passengers and crew be ready on deck.

12:25 AM: Lifeboats begin loading with women and children first. The *Carpathia* picks up distress calls and begins sailing toward *Titanic*.

12:45 AM: The first lifeboat is lowered with only twenty-eight people on board. The first distress rocket is fired.

2:05 AM: The last lifeboat is lowered while more than 1,500 people are left on the ship.

2:17 AM: The last radio message is sent.

2:20 AM: *Titanic* sinks into the Atlantic. People in the water floating in life preservers slowly freeze to death.

3:30 AM: Survivors spot the first rockets from *Carpathia*.

4:10 AM: *Carpathia* picks up the first lifeboat.

8:50 AM: *Carpathia* sets off from the *Titanic* rescue site for New York with 705 survivors.

April 18, 1912 *Carpathia* arrives in New York Harbor around 9 PM.

April 19, 1912 The US Senate's inquiry into the disaster begins.

April 22–May 15, 1912 A number of ships return to the disaster area and recover a total of 328 bodies. Many are buried at the Fairview Cemetery in Halifax, Nova Scotia.

May 2, 1912 The British Board of Trade inquiry into the disaster begins.

May 14, 1912 *Saved from the Titanic*, starring survivor Dorothy Gibson, opens in theaters.

November 1955 *A Night to Remember*, a nonfiction book by Walter Lord, is published. A film based on the book is released three years later.

September 1985 A team led by oceanographer Robert D. Ballard locates the *Titanic* wreck.

1986 Ballard returns to the site on a second expedition. Legal efforts begin to protect the wreck and restrict alteration and salvaging at the site.

1997 RMS Titanic, Inc. begins showing artifacts at several exhibits around the world. In December, James Cameron's blockbuster *Titanic* opens in theaters in the United States. The next year it wins eleven Academy Awards, tying *Ben-Hur* for the most Oscars won by a film.

1998 Chartered deep-sea excursions to the *Titanic* wreck site begin.

2012 Centennial commemorations of the disaster include the release of James Cameron's *Titanic* in 3D, orchestra performances of specially commissioned music, chartered theme cruises, TV miniseries, tribute postage stamps, and special exhibits, as well as the grand opening of Titanic Belfast—a museum that bills itself as the world's largest *Titanic* visitor attraction—in Ireland.

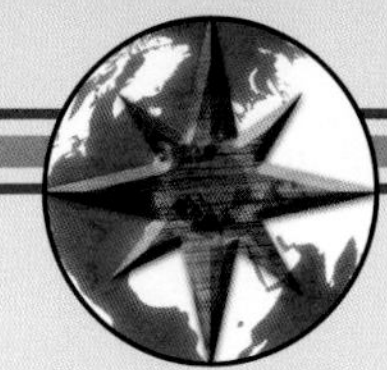

FOR FURTHER READING

Books

Robert Ballard and Rick Archbold, *The Discovery of the* Titanic. New York: Warner Books, 1988.

Steven Biel, *Down with the Old Canoe: A Cultural History of the* Titanic *Disaster*. New York: Norton, 1996.

John P. Eaton and Charles Haas, Titanic*: Destination Disaster—The Legends and the Reality*, third ed. Somerset, UK: Haynes Publishing, 2011.

Alastair Forsyth, Donald Hyslop, and Sheila Jemima, eds., Titanic *Voices: Memories from the Fateful Voyage*. New York: St. Martin's, 1997.

Jennifer Hooper McCarty and Tim Foecke, *What Really Sank the* Titanic. New York: Citadel, 2009.

Walter Lord, *A Night to Remember*. New York: Holt, Rinehart, and Winston, 1955.

Donald Lynch and Ken Marschall, Titanic*: An Illustrated History*. New York: Hyperion, 1995.

Wyn Craig Wade, *The* Titanic*: End of a Dream*. New York: Viking Penguin, 1986.

Periodicals and Internet Sources

David Ansen, "Our *Titanic* Love Affair," *Newsweek*, February 23, 1998.

Clarke Canfield, "Full *Titanic* Wreck Site Mapped for First Time," Associated Press, March 12, 2012.

Sean Coughlan, "*Titanic*: The Final Messages from a Stricken Ship," BBC News Magazine, April 9, 2012. www.bbc.com.

Sharon Gaudin, "*Titanic* Was a High-Tech Marvel of Its Time," *Computerworld*, April 13, 2012. www.computerworld.com.

Tony Hoffman, "How the *Titanic* Disaster Forever Changed Telecommunications," *PC Magazine*, April 2012. www.pcmag.com.

Verlyn Klinkenborg, "*Titanic* Repercussions," *American History Magazine*, April 2012.

Oceanus: *The International Magazine of Marine Science and Policy*, *The* Titanic*: Lost and Found*, vol. 28, no. 4, Winter 1985–1986. www.archive.org.

Clyde Sanger, "*Titanic*'s Wreck Found and Filmed," *The Guardian* (UK), September 3, 1985. www.theguardian.com.

"*Titanic* Sinks Four Hours After Hitting Iceberg," *New York Times*, April 15, 1912.

"The Wreck of the *Titanic* Now Protected by UNESCO," UNESCO, April 5, 2012. www.unesco.org.

Video

Lost Liners (PBS Home Video, 2000). This public television documentary examines four sunken ocean liners: *Titanic*; *Empress of Ireland*, a Canadian ship that sank after a collision in the Saint Laurence in 1914; *Lusitania*, which was sunk by a German U-boat during World War I; and *Britannic*, one of *Titanic*'s sister ships that was destroyed by an underwater mine while serving as a hospital ship in World War I. Thc program uses underwater images along with historical footage and includes commentary from historians and survivors. PBS also has a companion book (*Lost Liners: From the* Titanic *to the* Andrea Doria *the Ocean Floor Reveals Its Greatest Lost Ships* by Robert D. Ballard with illustrations by Ken Marschall) and a companion website (www.pbs.org/lostliners).

Titanic (directed by James Cameron, 1997). This Hollywood dramatization of the ship's maiden voyage won eleven Academy Awards, including best picture, and reigned as the highest grossing film of all time for more than a decade. The story focuses on the fictional romance of a woman traveling in first class and an immigrant in steerage. The movie incorporates underwater footage of the decaying wreck and realistic reconstructions of the ship and its opulent interiors.

Titanic: Death of a Dream (A&E Television Networks, 1994). This four-hour documentary explores *Titanic*'s story from the beginning of construction through its sinking in the North Atlantic four years later. It features interviews with survivors and noteworthy *Titanic* historians.

Websites

RMS *Titanic*, Woods Hole Oceanographic Institution (www.whoi.edu/main/topic/titanic). This website provides access to multimedia offerings from the largest oceanographic research and education institution in the United States on the exploration of the *Titanic* wreck. It includes information on the ship and its legacy, footage of expeditions to the wreck, interviews with scientists, and links to magazine articles.

***Titanic*: 100 Years** (http://channel.nationalgeographic.com/channel/titanic-100-years). This channel on the *National Geographic* website has videos and documentaries on the ship and exploration to the wreck; interviews with and articles by explorer-in-residence Robert D. Ballard; interactive features on the ship's creation, interiors, and route; and links to the magazine's vast archive of *Titanic* articles.

Titanic Historical Society (www.titanic1.org). The society's website has a wealth of materials about the ship and White Star Line for any *Titanic* enthusiast. It also includes information on the society's events, the *Titanic Commutator* (the society's magazine), and the Titanic Museum in Indian Orchard, Massachusetts.

Titanic Inquiry Project (www.titanicinquiry.org). This website includes complete transcripts and facsimiles of the *Titanic* hearings and reports from the US Senate and at the British Board of Trade.

Unsinkable, Unimaginable, Unforgettable: The *Titanic* 100 Years Later (www.denverpost.com/titanic). This website of content from the *Denver Post* provides access to historical and contemporary news stories about the disaster, copies of original documents, a large photo collection, interactive timeline, and a map.

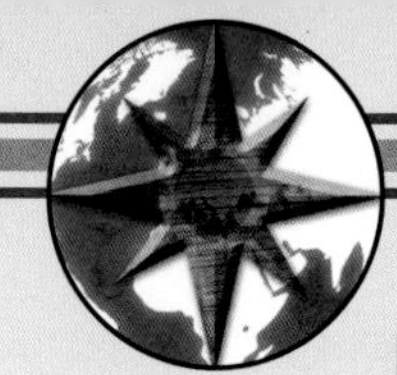

INDEX

A

Abandon Ship (film), 17
Abernathy, Lewis, 167
Academy Awards/Oscars, 21, 125
Adams, Stanley, 34
Akademik Mstislav Keldysh (Russian research vessel), 91, 165
Alvin (deep-sea submersible), 53–55, 84
Amerika (ship), ice warning to *Titanic*, 27, 33
ANGUS (Acoustically Navigated Geological Underwater Survey), 169
Archbold, Rick, 93
Argo (submersible robot), 50, 51–53, *55*
Artifacts of RMS *Titanic*
- appraised valuc, 60–61
- illegal plundering at site, 91
- post-1987 collection, 58–59, 60–61
- post-salvage lawsuits, 85–86
- Premier Exhibitions, Inc. ownership, 58–62
- pre-1987 collection, 59, 60–61
- recovery salvage, 8, 21
- US government conditions, 59–60

Asian (ship), wireless messages to *Titanic*, 37, 40
Astor, John Jacob, 16, 20, 48, 54, 120, 125, 150, 159
Athinai (ship), 33
Atlantic (film), 17

B

Ballard, Robert
- discovery of *Titanic* wreckage, 20–21, 49–56, 84
- evidence analysis, 54–55, 91, 92
- expedition planning, 51, 52
- post-discovery return to site, 53
- *PT-109* discovery, 56
- on *Titanic*'s deterioration, 91
- underwater technology innovation, 8, *55*, 56
- *Yorktown* discovery, 56

Beans, Edwards, 155–156
Bederman, David J., 61
Beesley, Lawrence, 16, 132
Bigham, Randy Bryan, 127
Books about *Titanic* tragedy, 20
Bride, Harold, 33, 34, 36, 38, 41, 72, *113*, 130
Britannic (ship), 105, 108
British Board of Trade, 30, 60, 110
British Mercantile Marines, 143
Broad, William J., 104–110
Bulletin machine technology, New York City, 43–44
Butt, Archibald W., 114

C

Cameron, James
- comment on crew dedication, 167
- 3D *Titanic* film, 123, 165–166
- *Titanic* site expedition, 165–169

wreck site dives, 87
See also Titanic (Cameron film)
Cameron, Michael, 165, 167
Canada, 86, 87, 88, 127
Cape Race, NL, 34, 37, 38, 39, 40
Carlisle, James Alexander, 108
Caronia (ship), wireless messages to *Titanic*, 33, 37, 38, 40
Cavalcade (play and film), 125–126
Cedric (ship), 115
Cherniev, Evgeny "Genya," 167
Clarke, J. Calvitt, 89
Construction of the *Titanic*
British Board of Trade permits, 60
bulkhead compartments inadequacies, 69–70
inadequate testing, training, 65–66
metal fracture analysis, 109
mistakes of ship designers, 100–103
naval architecture, 24–25, 101
passenger accommodations, 26–27
rivet quality, 106
rivet safety, 105
size safety factors, 26–27
theoretical sinking resistance, 24–25
unrestricted cost availability, 65
watertight construction, 24–25
See also Harland and Wolff shipbuilders; Rivets used in building *Titanic*
Control and Catastrophe in Human Affairs (McNeill), 98–99
The Convergence of the Twain (Hardy), 125
Cooper, Tilghman S., 117–119
Cornell, Robert C., 48
Corpse recovery, 157, 159, *160*, 162
Costa Concordia (cruise ship) disaster, 98, *98*, 101–103
Coward, Noël, 125
Cullimore, Roy, 93
Cultural resonance of *Titanic* tragedy
contemporaneous public response, 14–17
illumination of class distinctions, 15–16
initial media coverage, 14
limited post-tragedy interest, 17
religious leaders' response, 14–15
renewed post-tragedy interest, 17, 20, 22
Titanic (Cameron film), 21–22, 87, 123, 133, 166–167
Cunard shipping line, 107, 130
Cussler, Clive, 20

D

Davino, Christopher, 61
Deep-sea research advances, 55–56
Delgado, James, 59
Deutschland (oil tanker), 33
DiCaprio, Leonardo, 22
Dion, Celine, 22
Discovery Channel (TV network), 87
The Discovery of the Titanic (Ballard and Archbold), 93
Discovery of *Titanic* wreckage
Alvin/Jason Jr., missions, 53–55
Argo findings, 50, 51–53, *55*
Ballard, Robert, co-leadership, 20–21, 49–56, 84
deep-sea research advances, 55–56
future plans, 61–62
hundredth anniversary, 98
IFREMER Institute, 20, 50, 84, 85
location discovery challenges, 51
Michel, Jean Louis, co-leadership, 20, 50
resulting lawsuits, 83–89

Discovery of *Titanic* wreckage (*continued*)
rules for wreck site management, 88–89
SAR findings, 51–53
scheduled visits, 91, 94
sonar view images, 94–95, *95*
3D video recording gear, 62
UNESCO protection, 92
wreck site film footage, 60
Distress calls, initial, 34–35
Dobby, J.G., 48
Dodge, Washington, 156
Down to Eternity (O'Connor), 17

E

Earthship Productions, 165
Eastland (excursion ship) disaster, 101
Eaton, Jack, 92
Elia, Ricardo, 83–89
Elwood (ROV), 166–167
Evacuation of passengers from *Titanic*
chaos during, 140–142
discipline of crew, 143
Jessup, Violet, description, 148–152
jumping off ship, 142–143
route confusion, 102
Smith, Edward, delays, 102, 103
social class divisions, 116–121, 123, 125

F

Fellowes, Julian, 127
Final wireless messages of *Titanic*, 32–41
Finding Dorothy (Bigham), 127
First-class passengers, 119, 120, 137, 159, 162
Floodwaters, 100
Foecke, Tim, 93, 106, 108, 109–110
Force, W.H., 48
Forensic naval architecture, 101
France
aid in search for *Titanic*, 20, 50, 84, 85
Titanic agreement discussions, 86, 87, 88
US Department of State contact, 84
Frankfurt (ship) wireless messages to *Titanic*, 35, 38, 40
Franklin, P.A.S., 45–48
Freeman, Ernest, 163
Fulford, Robert, 122–127
Futility (Robertson), 17

G

Ghosts of the Abyss (documentary), 160
Gibson, Dorothy, 16, 123, 126–128
Global response to *Titanic* tragedy, 14–17
Globe Newswire, 57–62
Gordon, Sir Cosmo Edmund Duff, 139
Gracie, Archibald, 72, 132
Grand Trunk Railway system, 119
Great Yarmouth Radio Club, 32–41
Gregg, Jill A., 13–22
Griggs, John W., 115
Grimes, Tammy, 20
Guggenheim, Benjamin, 16, 120, 125

H

Haas, Charles, 92
Haddock, Captain, 47–48
Hall, Norman, 20
Halomonas titanicae bacteria, 93
Hardy, Thomas, 125
Harland and Wolff shipbuilders
absence of cost limitations, 65
Belfast, Ireland shipyard, *25*

Ireland archives office, 110
shipyard during *Titanic* construction, *25*
use of central hull only, 107–108
use of low quality rivets, 105, 106
Harris, G. Michael, 89
Harris, Henry, 132
Harris, Rene, 132
Hartley, Wallace, 161
Hays, Charles M., 119
History Channel (TV network), 94
House of Lords, UK Parliament, 75–82
Hume, Jock, 159–160, 162–163
Hurricane Danielle, 95
Hurricane Earl, 95
Hurricane Igor, 95

I

Ice field warnings, 27, 33–34, 67–68
IFREMER Institute (France), 20, 50, 84, 85
IMAX film expedition, 93
Immigrants
anti-foreign feelings, 121
control of Slavic immigrants, 120
negative assumptions about, 6
as revenue source, 118
Institute of Nautical Archaeology, 94
International Ice Patrol, 16, 101
International law and jurisdiction issues, 75–82
International Mercantile Marine Company, 45, 65
International Navigation Co. (Ltd.), 65
Investigation of *Titanic* disaster
Earl of Halsbury, testimony, 82
international law and jurisdiction, 75–82
justification of US inquiry, 77–79
Lord St. Davids, testimony, 82
Marquess of Lansdowne, testimony, 80–81
Morley, John, testimony, 79–80
necessity of US inquiry, 79–81
Stanhope, Earl, testimony, 76–77
US Navy, 52
US Senate committee, 27, *66*, 113–115
Ireland
first voyage departure, 14
Harland and Wolff archives, 105, 110
Titanic construction, *25*, 65
Ismay, J. Bruce
anger directed against, 130–131
help in loading lifeboats, 141
saving of own life, 161
Senate testimony, 27, 65

J

Jake (ROV), 167
Janssen, David, 20
Jason Jr. (deep-sea submersible), 53–56
Jean Charcot (research vessel), 94, 95
Jessup, Violet, 146–152
Johnston, Lori, 93
Josyln, John A., 86–87

K

Kaiser Wilhelm (ship), 117
Knorr (research vessel), 51
Kronprinz Wilhelm (ship), 100–101
Kudriashov, Sergey, 168

L

Lansdowne, Marquess of, 80–81
Launching of the *Titanic*, 65, 170

Lawsuits following *Titanic's* discovery
artifact salvage lawsuits, 85–86
international challenges, 86–88
Oceanic Steam Navigation Company payments, 84
rules for wreck site management, 88–89
Lee, Paul, 90–96
Lifeboats
American and British laws, 16
boarding process, 154–155, 156, 157
capacity decisions, 67, 70, 73, 101, 125, 161–162
Carpathia rescue, *139*
dimensions and locations, *71*
Olympic crew incident over, 161–162
Smith, Edward, orders, 70, 102, 103
social class distinctions, 119
survivor reports, 72
Titanic wreck site and, 50
Lightoller, Charles, 68, 72
Livingstone, David, 108
London Steamship and Indemnity Association, 85
Long, Milton, 139, 140, 142
Lord, Walter, 17
The Loss of the S.S. Titanic (Beesley), 16
Lusitania (ship), 107, 117
Lynch, Don, 167

M

Mackay-Bennett (ship), 159, 162
Marconi wireless apparatus
Carpathia's messages to *Titanic*, 112–113
final *Titanic* messages, 32–41
ice warnings from other ships to *Titanic*, 33, 38–40
loss of connection, 40–41
usage for distress signals, 16
use of SOS and CQD messages, 34–35, 36
Marconi Wireless Company of America, 112
Marex Titanic Inc., 85
Marschall, Ken, 164–169
Marsh, Ed, 166
Martin, Bradley, Jr., 48
Mass, William J., 44
Mauretania (ship), 117
McCarty, Jennifer Cooper, 105, 106–107, 110
McElroy, H.W., 141–142
McNeill, William H., 98–99
Medusa (lighting platform), 165
The Memory of Eva Ryker (Hall), 20
Metallurgical research on *Titanic's* rivets, 107–108
Michel, Jean-Louis, 20, 50
Minne, Joris, 108
Mir 1 and *2* (deep submersibles), 165, 166–167, 169
Morgan, J. Pierpont, 125
Morning Call (newspaper), 117
Mullin, Tom, 163
Murdoch, William McMaster, 68
My Heart Will Go On (song), 22

N

National Geographic (magazine), 20, 91
National Institute of Standards and Technology, 106, 109–110
National Maritime Museum (England), 86
National Oceanic Atmospheric Administration (NOAA), 59, 88, 89

Naval architecture, 24–25, 102
Naval engineering, 98, 100, 103, 106
Navratil, Michel, 131
Negligence causes of *Titanic* disaster, 64–74
New York Herald (newspaper), 111–115, 121
New York Navy Yard, 115
New York Post (newspaper), 153–157
New York Times (newspaper), 42–48
News/announcements of *Titanic* disaster
  behavior at White Star Line office, 48
  editorial cartoons, 121
  Franklin, P.A.S., public message, 45–46
  Haddock, Captain, message, 47–48
  heroism of first-class passengers, 120
  timeline of *Titanic's* messages, 46–48
  Times Square, New York, during, 43–44
A Night to Remember (film), 17, 123, 124
A Night to Remember (Lord), 17
NOAA (National Oceanic Atmospheric Administration), 59, 88, 89

O

Oceanic Steam Navigation Company, 65, 84
O'Connor, Richard, 17
Olympic (ship)
  construction, 65, 105, 118
  crew incident over lifeboats, 161–162
  incident-free career, 108
  use in *Titanic* movie, 16
  wireless messages with *Titanic*, 35–40, 46–48, 47
"Operation *Titanic*" (Deep Ocean Expeditions), 87
Oscars. *See* Academy Awards/Oscars
Osprey video camera, 165

P

Pace Technologies, 165
Panavision, 165
Panic of 1873, 99
Phillips, John George, 33, 34, 36, 38, 40–41, 72
Phoenix Engineering, 165
Pirrie, Lord William, 106
P.P. Shirshov Institute of Oceanology, 168
Pratt, E.J., 125
Premier Exhibitions, Inc., 58–62

R

Raise the Titanic (Cussler), 20
Rappahannock (ship), ice warning to *Titanic*, 33
Religious leaders' response, 14–15
Reynolds, Debbie, 20
Rheins, George, 156–157
River levees, 100
Rivets used in building *Titanic*
  best vs. best-best quality, 106
  challenge to findings, 108–109
  irony of flawed rivets, 109–110
  metallurgical research, 107–108
  questions about safety, 105
  recovery of rivets, 105–106
  research on shortage, 105–106
  use of low quality rivets, 105, 106
RMS *Californian* (ship), 33, 34, 90, 103
RMS *Carpathia* (ship)
  arrival in New York Harbor, 126
  request to withhold details, 112–113
  rescue of *Titanic* survivors, 50, 72, 112–113, *113*, 126, 130, 132, *139*, 154–156
  Senate investigation, 66, 115
  wireless messages, 30, 35, 40, 41

RMS Titanic, Inc. (RMST), 58, 61–62, 85, 91, 94, 96
RMS *Titanic* Maritime Memorial Act, 84
Robertson, Morgan, 17
Robinson, Tony, 93
ROVs (remotely operated vehicles), 165–167
Russia
  Academy of Sciences, 168
  Akademik Mstislav (research vessel), 91, 165
  deep sea submersibles, 87, 91, 165, 166–169

S

Sammis, T.W., 112–114
SAR sonar search vehicle, 51–53
Saved from the Titanic (silent film), 16, 123, 125–126
Science and Its Times (encyclopedia), 49–55
Scientific American (magazine), 16, 23–31
Search for the Titanic (video game), 21
Secrets of the Titanic (documentary), 20
Shipwrecks in the media, 14
Sims, Philip, 101
Sinking of the *Titanic*
  aid from other ships, 38–40
  breakup sequence, *29*
  corpse recovery, 157, 159, *160*, 162
  fatal blow, 28
  flaws in rivets and, 104–110
  iceberg collision and damage, 68–69
  ignored ice field warnings, 27, 33–34, 67–68
  inadequate pre-launch testing, training, 65–66
  initial distress calls, 34–35
  lifeboat issues, 30–31, 67, 70, 73, 101, 125, 161–162
  loss of wireless connection, 40–41
  negligence causes, 64–74
  Olympic's communication during, 36–37
  post-disaster government recommendations, 72–74
  religious leaders' response, 14–15
  theoretical built-in resistance, 24–25
  wind and weather conditions, 26
  See also Evacuation of passengers; Survivor accounts
Sisson, Wade, 129–134
Size of the *Titanic*, 14, 26–27
Smith, Edward
  doubts about sinking possibility, 100
  Franklin, P.A.S., messages, 45–48
  giving of testimony, 68
  instructions to crew, 41
  misuse of lifeboats, 70
  Oceanic ocean crossings, 117
  reckless speed of *Titanic*, 27
  wireless distress messages, 33, 34, 37, 38
Sony, 165
S.O.S. Titanic (TV miniseries), 20
Special-effects-miniatures sequences, 166
S.S. *Antillian* (ship), 33
S.S. *Baltic* (ship), 33, 37, 38, 46, 67, 117
S.S. *Mesaba* (ship), 33–34
Stanhope, Earl, 76–77
Stanwyck, Barbara, 17
Stehle, Max Frohlicher, 154–155
Strauss, Ida, 15
Le Suroit (research vessel), 51
Survivor accounts
  accusations of cowardice, 130–131
  Beans, Edwards, 155–156
  Beesley, Lawrence, 16, 132

Brown, Tobin, 20
Dean, Millvina, 133
Dodge, Washington, 156
Evans, Edith, 130
Hawksford, W.J., 157
Jessup, Violet, 146–152
post-disaster communication, 132
Rheins, George, 156–157
shared escape stories, 153–157
Stehle, Max Frohlicher, 154–155
Thayer, Jack, 133–134, 136–145
Titanic "waifs," 131

T

Tacoma Narrows Bridge (WA), 100
Taft, William Howard, 114
Tenner, Edward, 97–103
Thayer, John B. "Jack," 72, 133–134, 136–145
Third-class passengers, 72, 117, 119–120, 151
3D images catalogue, 94
3D video recording gear, 62, 165
The Time Tunnel (TV show), 20
Times Square, New York City, 43–44
Titanic (Cameron film), 8, 21–22, 87, 123, 133, 166–167
Titanic (German film), 17
Titanic (1953 film), 17
The Titanic (Pratt), 125
Titanic (teleplay), 17
Titanic (UK/Canada miniseries), 127
Titanic: A New Musical, 21
Titanic Historical Society, 109, 133
Titanic International Society, 92
Titanic: Triumph and Tragedy (Eaton and Haas), 92–93
Titanic Ventures, 85
La Touraine (ship), ice warning to *Titanic*, 33
Trower, Tim, 109
The Truth About the Titanic (Gracie), 132
Turnbull, Ann, 150, 151, 152

U

UNESCO (United Nations Educational, Scientific, and Cultural Organization), 92
United Kingdom (UK)
claimant compensation requests, 84
Titanic agreement discussions, 86, 87, 88
United States (US)
inspection certificates, 72–73
justification for inquiry, 77–79
necessity for inquiry, 79–81
RMS *Titanic* Maritime Memorial Act, 84
Titanic agreement discussions, 86, 87, 88
Wireless Ship Act Amendment, 39
United States Attorney, 59
The Unsinkable Molly Brown (musical and film), 20
US Department of Commerce, 59
US Department of State, 84, 89
US Senate Committee on Commerce, 64–74
US Senate Investigating Committee, 27, 66, 113–115
USA Today (newspaper), 102

V

Vassalos, Dracos, 102
Virginian (ship), wireless messages to *Titanic*, 37, 38, 40, 41, 46

W

Waitt Institute for Discovery, 94
Ward, Christopher, 158–163
Webb, Clifton, 17
What Really Sank the Titanic? (Foecke), 93, 108
Whelan, Frank, 116–121
White Star Line
  apologetic advertisements, 161
  behavior at New York City offices, *47*, 48
  brochure description of *Titanic*, 109
  construction of sister ships, 110, 118
  encouraging messages, 45–46
  Senate testimony, 27, 115
Widener, George, 119
Wind and weather conditions, 26
Winkleman, Sophie, 127
Winslet, Kate, 22
Wireless messages. *See* Final wireless messages of *Titanic*
Wireless operators of *Titanic*
  missed ice warnings, 33
  receipt of ice warnings, 27, 67
  Senate investigation, *66*, 113–115
  withholding information for profit, 111–115
Wireless Ship Act Amendment (1912), 39
Woods Hole Oceanographic Institute, 20, 50, 84, 94, 169
Wreck site film footage, 60

Y

You Are There (TV show), 17

Z

Zegrahm Expeditions, 89